My
Big
Fat
Greek
Feast

D1295761

My Big Fat Greek Feast

small potatoes press

Design: Connie Correia Fisher
Copy edit: Joanne Correia
Reseach: Crystal Callahan

ISBN: 0-9749617-0-1
Library of Congress Control Number: 2004101209

Small Potatoes Press
401 Collings Avenue
Collingswood, NJ 08108
856-869-5207

Visit us on the Web!
www.smallpotatoespress.com

Printed in the United States

Dedications

I would like to dedicate this book to three important people in my life:

To my wife: Frances
She is the light in my life.
She is the one who encourages me to do everything, no matter what the cost.
She is the one who tells me honestly how my cooking, how my creations, really are.
She stands by me, she is a part of me.

To my father: Evangelos (Angelo)
He is the one who pushes me and teaches me.
He is one of the greatest chefs I know.
I have learned and will continue to learn a lot from the man I call Dad.

To my grandfather: George Skordos
He was one of the most talented chefs to ever live.
I only wish he was still around to see what I have become,
to see what I have learned from him and
how I have used the talent he helped pass on to me.

Table of Contents

Introduction

GREEK CUISINE

Greek cuisine has a great variety of dishes and can be an extremely satisfying culinary adventure for everyone's tastes. Greece is a country with a long history, a country which gave birth to philosophers and architects and even cooks. Greece's culinary tradition has a span of over 4,000 years. In fact, it was Archestratos in 330 B.C., who wrote the first cookbook.

Traditional Greek cuisine differs from other cuisines because it is a combination of its entire environment. Greece has fresh, unique ingredients and a philosophy of eating and sharing meals. The Greek meal experience is unlike any other.

GREECE'S INGREDIENTS

The secret of Greek cuisine is the fresh meats and fish, the abundance of great herbs and spices, and don't forget the best olive oil in the world.

The mild Greek climate allows most fruits and vegetables to be grown naturally, full of aroma and flavor. Many Greeks collect fresh herbs from their mountains and countryside. These herbs are legendary for their taste and scent. A little bit of fresh picked herbs, such as oregano, thyme, dill, or rosemary, will add an immeasurable depth to the flavors of traditional Greek dishes.

The seafood from the crystal clear Mediterranean and Aegean Seas is incomparable to inferior seafood caught in the vast oceans. Chickens, lambs, and goats in Greece are free-grazing creatures that have a unique taste not to be found on any farm.

THE GREEK PHILOSOPHY

Sharing small meals or appetizers "*mezedes*" around a table with friends, either at home or in a restaurant or a *taverna*, is an all-embracing tradition that Greeks enjoy. Greek *tavernas* have a comfortable and laid-back atmosphere, but the food preparation is a timeless tradition that is passed down through generations.

COOKING IN THE EYES OF GEORGE

A good cook is one who can take a recipe and makes it his/her own. If a recipe is too salty or too sweet, he/she will adjust the recipe accordingly.

A good cook is also one who knows how to substitute. Substitution is simply taking out one ingredient and adding another. Substitution is the key to good cooking or being a good cook. Don't be afraid to experiment and substitute. If a dish calls for ground lamb, substitute ground chicken; if a recipe calls for cilantro, use a flat-leaf parsley. Just because you don't have a certain ingredient, don't just disregard a recipe—substitute!

Cooking is not about following a recipe. Cooking is not about being able to make some key dishes. Cooking is about something called passion. Passion is the feeling that you have when you're cooking: it's that love for the art, the love for the process and the finished product.

As Julia Child once said, "Cooking is not a chore, it is a joy." It has always been for me and I hope I can share this joy with you.

Enjoy!

George Kyrtatas

Meze

Stuffed Grape Leaves
"Dolmathes"

Dolmathes are not only a great appetizer, they are also a distinct topping on the famous Greek salad. The great thing about dolmathes is that you can make a large amount, submerge them in oil, and then store them in the refrigerator. They never go bad; and whenever I want one, I just open the Tupperware and take as many as I want. Can't go wrong with this one.

1 cup olive oil

3 onions, finely chopped

2 bunches scallions, finely chopped

2 cups cooked rice

⅓ cup finely chopped parsley

1 teaspoon finely chopped dill

1 tablespoon salt

2 lemons

1 (16-ounce) jar grape leaves

2½ cups water

Heat oil in a pan. Add onions and scallions and sauté until transparent, approximately 5 minutes. Add rice and sauté with onions and scallions for another minute. Add parsley, dill, salt, and juice of both lemons. Simmer and stir for 5 minutes. Remove from fire and let sit until mixture is cool enough to handle.

While waiting for mixture to cool, prepare the grape leaves for stuffing. To do this, rinse the grape leaves and lay them on paper towel with the dull side of the grape leaf up.

Place a teaspoon of the mixture in the center of each grape leaf. Fold in all corners of the leaf, then roll into a cigar shape. (Be careful not to roll the grape leaf too tightly because the leaf will rip as the rice expands. But don't roll the leaf too loose either because the filling will fall out.)

Preheat oven to 350°. When all dolmathes are rolled, place them in the bottom of a pot. Arrange them tightly to help ensure they do not fall apart on you. Fill the pot with the water and cover. Place in the oven and cook until all the water is all absorbed or until rice is soft. (More water might be needed, depending on what pot is used.)

If not serving right away, submerge grape leaves in additional olive oil and refrigerate. Serve cold or at room temperature.

Yields approximately 50 pieces

Greek Baguette with a Sweet Kiss

I first came up with this recipe one night when I wanted to make garlic bread to serve with a pasta dinner. The only problem was I had no garlic in the house, so I just started throwing things on a piece of bread. That mixture came to be the base for this recipe. I fine-tuned it, and now it is a great little appetizer. If you are feeling adventurous, you can make the bread from scratch.

1 French baguette, cut into 10 slices

2 tablespoons honey

1 teaspoon cayenne pepper

1 teaspoon paprika

½ teaspoon brown sugar

1 (20 ounce) can figs packed in water, drained and sliced into small pieces

4 ounces Gorgonzola cheese, crumbled

Arrange baguette slices on a sheet tray. Evenly spread honey on each slice. Combine cayenne pepper, paprika, and brown sugar and sprinkle over honey. Top with figs and Gorgonzola.

Broil until cheese begins to melt. Plate and serve warm.

Yields 10 slices

Big Fat Greek Fact

According to legend, the Greek goddess Demeteria was the first to show figs to mortals. She called it the "fruit of autumn." Every inhabitant of Athens, including Plato, was a *philosykos,* "a friend of the fig." Mithridates, the Greek King of Pontus, considered figs to be an antidote for all sickness and pains. He ordered his doctors to use them medicinally and his citizens to consume them daily. Figs were used as a training food by the early Olympic athletes, and were also presented as laurels to the winners — first Olympic "medal."

Spanakopita

Spanakopita is a cheese and spinach pie wrapped in phyllo. I think it's a great first course or side dish. Serve it as a meatless entree with a green salad.

¼ cup water

1 (10-ounce) package frozen chopped spinach

2 teaspoons olive oil

½ cup chopped scallion

2 cloves garlic, minced

4 ounces feta cheese, crumbled

3 ounces cottage cheese

1 tablespoon chopped dill

¼ teaspoon pepper

⅓ teaspoon salt

8 sheets frozen phyllo dough, thawed

1 stick butter, melted

Preheat oven to 350°.

Bring water to a boil. Add spinach, cover, and boil until spinach is defrosted. Place spinach in a colander and drain until barely moist. Set aside.

Heat oil in pan over medium-high heat. Add scallions and garlic and sauté until scallions are soft. Add the spinach, feta, cottage cheese, dill, pepper, and salt. Stir to combine and remove from heat.

Place 1 phyllo sheet on a buttered sheet pan. (Cover remaining dough to keep from drying out.) Lightly coat sheet with melted butter. Coat 3 more phyllo sheets, one at a time, with melted butter and stack one on top of the other.

Spoon spinach mixture on top of the phyllo dough and spread evenly.

Brush remaining phyllo dough with butter and place on top of spinach mixture, making sure to press the phyllo down firmly. Score the top phyllo into a triangle shaped piece and butter the top of the phyllo.

Bake for 35 minutes or until golden brown. Cut into triangles. Serve warm.

Yields approximately 20 triangles

Spinach, Sun-dried Tomato, and Goat Cheese Pita Pizzas

A lighter "white" pizza can be made by eliminating the tomato paste and sugar and putting the other ingredients directly on the pizza. Just add a little more olive oil.

½ cup tomato paste

¼ teaspoon dried oregano

¼ teaspoon salt

⅛ teaspoon sugar

½ cup olive oil

2 large pita bread rounds

3 cups torn spinach

2 cups sun-dried tomato halves

2 fresh basil leaves, torn

1 clove garlic, sliced

½ cup chevre or goat cheese (Feta can be substituted.)

Combine tomato paste, oregano, salt, and sugar in a small bowl.

Lightly oil pita breads and place on a sheet pan. Lightly broil pita until it gets a little crispy. Remove from broiler.

Top with sauce mixture. Then layer on spinach, sun-dried tomatoes, basil, garlic, and cheese. Broil until cheese starts to melt.

Yields 2 pizzas

Big Fat Greek Fact

Mezedes — small, savory plates of food enjoyed in a friendly, relaxed atmosphere — encompass the whole Mediterranean culture and are one of Greece's basic dining experiences. The tradition of *meze* traces its roots to the beginnings of recorded history. Almost anything can be served as a *meze*, from a simple plate of olives to the recipes in this chapter. Aim for variety and a contrast of flavors, textures, and spices.

Fiery Fried Cheese
"Saganaki"

Guests will be impressed with this famous Greek dish. Just make sure you serve it immediately. It must be eaten hot and right away to avoid a rubbery texture. Cut into wedges or just dig right in with sesame crackers, wedges of pita, cocktail rye bread or crackers.

⅓ pound kasseri cheese
1 tablespoon butter
1 tablespoon vegetable oil
1 tablespoon Metaxa Cognac
1 lemon

Cut cheese into slices or cubes, depending on what you prefer.

Melt butter and oil in a frying pan. (Butter alone can be used; but when you use half butter and half oil, the cheese stays a lighter golden color rather then turning a darker brown.)

Put cheese into frying pan and cook until golden brown and crusty on all sides.

Remove from oil and place on a serving plate. Pour Metaxa over cheese and ignite. Immediately squeeze lemon juice over cheese.

Serves 2 to 4

Big Fat Greek Fact

Kasseri is a Greek cheese usually made from sheep's or goat's milk. After the curd is warmed, it is hand stretched and kneaded, then put into molds. The cheese rounds are placed in special aging rooms for six months. The flavor continues to develop and improve even after it has been packed. Kasseri is a hard cheese with a creamy gold color and a sharp, salty flavor.

Fried Feta and Zucchini Patties

I like to take these patties and freeze them after they are fried. Then whenever I know guests are coming over, I take them out of the freezer, defrost them slowly in the refrigerator, and then heat them in the oven. What a nice, easy way to be prepared for company without a lot of work.

1 pound zucchini, grated

1 teaspoon kosher salt

1 cup crumbled feta cheese

2 tablespoons grated fresh Parmesan cheese

4 tablespoons flour

2 eggs, beaten

2 cloves garlic, minced

2 scallions, sliced thin

1 tablespoon finely chopped dill

1 teaspoon chopped mint

Pepper to taste

Vegetable oil for frying

Place zucchini on a plate and sprinkle with kosher salt. (This will help remove the moisture.) Set aside for a maximum of 5 minutes. Rinse with cold water and strain in colander. Then wrap in a paper towel and squeeze until all the water is removed.

Place zucchini and all remaining ingredients, except oil, in a bowl and fold carefully to combine. Form mixture into patties about the size of the palm of your hand.

Heat oil in a large pan over medium-high heat. Sauté patties until golden brown on each side. Handle carefully when turning or patty will fall apart.

Serves 8 to 10

Fried Eggplant and Zucchini
"Melitzanes ke Kolokithia Tiganita"

This is one of my wife's favorite appetizers. When we went to Greece we would get this before each meal with a side of tzaziki sauce for dipping. WOW!

2 small eggplant, cut paper thin
4 small zucchini, cut paper thin
4 cups flour
Vegetable oil for frying

Soak vegetable slices in a bowl of salted water for 30 minutes. (This will help remove water from vegetables.) Remove vegetables from water and dredge in flour.

Heat oil in a medium-size frying pan over high heat. Fry vegetables until golden brown. Remove from oil and place on paper towels to drain.

Serves 6 to 8 (2, if one of them is me)

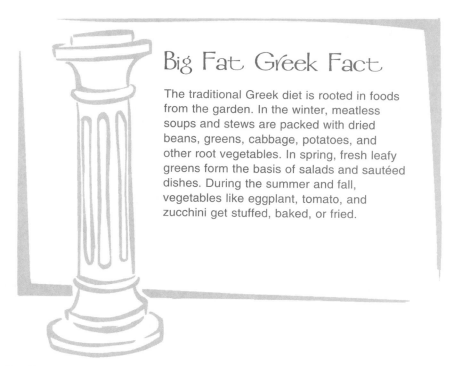

Big Fat Greek Fact

The traditional Greek diet is rooted in foods from the garden. In the winter, meatless soups and stews are packed with dried beans, greens, cabbage, potatoes, and other root vegetables. In spring, fresh leafy greens form the basis of salads and sautéed dishes. During the summer and fall, vegetables like eggplant, tomato, and zucchini get stuffed, baked, or fried.

Greek Meatballs

"Keftethakia"

When I was about twelve years old, I would watch my grandmother from the loft in her house as she made her meatballs. I would wait until she was finished frying the first batch so I could sneak downstairs and steal a handful. For some reason there would never be enough meatballs at dinner time. As the years went by, I realized that she had always known about my pilfering, but acted like she had no idea.

2 pounds ground beef

1 cup finely chopped onion

2 cloves garlic, minced

2 cups breadcrumbs, moistened (fresh white bread preferred)

2 eggs

1 tablespoon each salt and pepper

2 tablespoons chopped parsley

½ tablespoon chopped mint

Flour for dredging

Vegetable oil for frying

Combine all ingredients, except flour and oil, in a bowl. Use your hands to mix well. Roll into bite-size balls and dredge in flour.

Heat oil in a frying pan over high heat. Fry meatballs in cooking oil until brown and cooked inside.

Yields 16 to 20 meatballs

Fried Mussels
"Midia Tiganita"

For a nice salad serve mussels over baby arugula and top with crumbled feta cheese and Greek salad dressing. When selecting mussels in their shells, look for tightly closed shells or shells that snap shut when tapped. Smaller mussels are more tender than larger ones.

1 pound mussels meat (mussels removed from shells)

2 cups seasoned breadcrumbs

Vegetable oil for frying

Greek Salad Dressing (Recipe appears on page 43.)

Dredge mussels in breadcrumbs.

Heat oil in a medium-size frying pan over high heat. Fry mussels until golden brown.

Top with Greek salad dressing.

Serves 4 to 8 as an appetizer
Serves 1 to 2 as an entree

Fried Smelt
"Marides Tiganites"

I had this dish for the first time in Greece when I was 16 years old. I didn't want to eat it. My grandfather begged me to try, but I refused. When the platter was almost gone, he asked me one more time, and I finally tasted one. I was then upset with myself because I missed out on a great appetizer.

1 pound smelt or any other small fish

3 cups flour

Vegetable oil for frying

2 lemons

1 tablespoon salt

¼ cup chopped parsley

Wash smelt under cold water. Dredge in flour.

Heat oil in a medium-size frying pan over a medium-high heat. Fry smelt in oil until golden brown.

Squeeze lemon over smelt and sprinkle with salt and parsley.

Serves 2 to 4

Octopus on the Grill
"Octopothi sti Plaka"

If you put a little baking soda on octopus the night before and refrigerate, this will help to soften the meat. This is a tedious recipe to make, but it has great results.

2 1-pound whole octopus, cleaned with ink sac and beak removed

3 lemons, halved

4 tablespoons extra virgin olive oil

4 tablespoons dried oregano

2 tablespoons balsamic vinegar

1 teaspoon kosher salt

½ cup diced tomato

½ cup pitted and chopped kalamata olives

Bring salted water to a boil in a large pot. Squeeze in the juice of one lemon and put rind in water.

Hold tentacles with tongs and dip into boiling water until the tentacles curl. (This is done so the suctions do not stick to the pot.) Submerge octopus in water and cook for 30 minutes.

Meanwhile, mix remaining lemon juice, olive oil, oregano, balsamic vinegar, and kosher salt in a large bowl. Add diced tomatoes and olives.

Remove octopus from water and put on a hot grill. Reduce grill heat from high to medium and grill for 5 minutes on each side. Remove from grill and cut the octopus into pieces.

Transfer to a platter. (Try to keep the octopus form for a better plate presentation.) Top with prepared mixture.

Serves 2 to 4

Dips
and Chips

Mediterranean Pita Chips

If you are having a party, you must have these pita chips. They will replace the bread that is usually served to dip into a number of sauces. You can even make little pita pizza chips by drizzling them with tomato sauce and melting some mozzarella cheese on top.

3 large pita bread rounds

2 tablespoons melted butter

3 teaspoons grated Parmesan cheese

2 teaspoons dried oregano

2 teaspoons dried basil

1 teaspoon granulated garlic

¾ teaspoon paprika

Cut pita bread into triangle pieces and lay on a cookie sheet. Brush pita triangles with melted butter.

Combine all dry ingredients in a bowl and mix. Evenly sprinkle mixture over pita triangles.

Preheat oven to 350°. Place pita in oven and bake for 5 minutes or until pita is toasted.

Serves 4

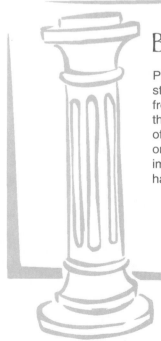

Big Fat Greek Fact

Pitas tend to become hard once dry, so try storing them in a plastic bag to prevent them from drying out. When you're ready to use the pitas, simply heat them in a small amount of olive oil in a shallow skillet for one minute on each side. Make sure you use the pitas immediately after heating so they do not harden again.

Chickpea Spread with Sesame Paste

"Hummus bi Tahini"

The debate goes on: Is hummus Greek or Lebanese or Arabic or what? Who cares! Whether you spell it hoummos, homus, or humus, this delicious dip is now popular all over the world. I like hummus best served with fresh toasted pita chips or crisp crudité.

3 cups canned chickpeas,
 drained and rinsed

3 cloves garlic, minced fine

½ teaspoon each salt and
 white pepper

2 lemons, juice only

2 tablespoons tahini

½ cup extra virgin olive oil

Combine chickpeas, garlic, and salt and pepper in a food processor and chop on high speed. With motor running, add lemon juice and tahini. Slowly add olive oil and continue to mix until the chickpeas are smooth and without lumps.

Yields 4 cups

Asiago Cheese and Kalamata Dip

This dish is one of my favorite party dishes. For a great presentation, serve it in a fondue pot covered with Parmesan cheese and some breadcrumbs. Brown the top a little with a cooking torch. To really impress your guests, pour half a shot of brandy on top and light it on fire. Serve with Mediterranean pita chips rather than traditional breads or chips.

⅓ cup crumbled feta cheese

¼ cup finely chopped parsley

¼ cup pitted and chopped kalamata olives

¼ cup finely chopped pimentos

14 ounces sour cream

6 ounces Asiago cheese, grated

1 teaspoon granulated garlic

½ cup breadcrumbs

¼ cup Parmesan cheese

Preheat oven to 350°.

Mix first 7 ingredients in a bowl. Transfer to an oven-proof casserole dish. Sprinkle with breadcrumbs and Parmesan cheese. Bake until the mixture is golden brown on top and just beginning to bubble, about 30 minutes.

Yields 4 cups

Feta Cheese Relish

A relish isn't just something you put on fish. A relish, and especially this one, can be added to a number of dishes ranging from meat and poultry to finger sandwiches. Just try the recipe once, then use your imagination as to what you want to put it on.

1 cup crumbled feta cheese
½ cup pitted and chopped kalamata olives
3 tablespoons olive oil
2 tablespoons lemon juice
½ teaspoon sugar
½ teaspoon honey
Salt and pepper to taste

Mix all ingredients together and refrigerate.

Yields 2 cups

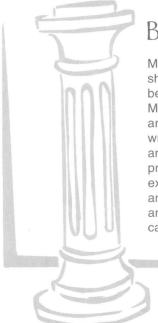

Big Fat Greek Fact

Most of the cheese in Greece is made from sheep or goat milk. Shepherding has always been a way of life in the Greek countryside. Many of the simple cheeses produced today are almost indistinguishable from those written about thousands of years ago. In ancient times cheese was the main dairy product: milk and butter were much more expensive. Ancient chefs melted, smoked, and toasted cheese and used it to add flavor and substance to sauces, breads, and cakes.

Garlic Spread
"Skordalia"

Use caution when eating this dip. The garlic aroma is very strong. If you want to have friends, only eat a little!

1 head garlic, peeled and minced or pressed

2 cups mashed potatoes, approximately 4 potatoes

4 slices white bread, crusts removed, moistened, and squeezed dry

⅓ cup lemon juice

Salt and pepper to taste

1 cup olive oil

Place garlic and mashed potatoes in a food processor and pulse slowly. Add bread, lemon juice, and spices. Continue to pulse.

Turn processor to high. With motor running, slowly pour in olive oil. Continue to pour in olive oil until a nice smooth spread is made. (You don't need to use all the oil once you reach a consistency you like. It's ok if some oil is left over.)

Yields 6 cups

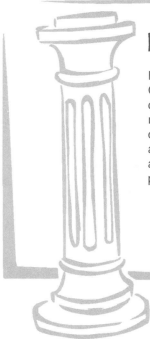

Big Fat Greek Fact

Not only is olive oil the primary fat used in Greek cooking, it is fundamental to Greek culture and identity. It is tied to every religious ritual and folk tradition that mark the crucial events in the cycle of life. Infants are anointed with olive oil at their christening, and olive oil is part of the embalming procedure prior to burial.

Fish Roe Spread
"Taramasalata"

Taramasalata is a versatile appetizer with a rich, smoky flavor. Casually, you can offer it with pita chips and olives. For something more fancy, serve it as an hors d'oeuvre on rye toast and garnish with parsley and capers.

1 (10-ounce) jar tarama (fish roe)

1 loaf Italian bread, crusts removed, bread moistened and squeezed dry

1 cup lemon juice

1 teaspoon white pepper

20 ounces vegetable oil

Place tarama in an electric mixer and beat on high. (This is done to break the eggs and to release the flavor inside.) Break bread into pieces and add to the eggs. Add lemon juice and white pepper.

While mixing on high, slowly add the vegetable oil, stopping periodically in order to make a good emulsion.

Add oil until a light, fluffy spread is made. (Depending on the consistency you prefer, some oil may be left over or more might be needed.)

Yields approximately 10 cups

Garlic Cucumber Dip
"Tzaziki"

Serve this classic Greek dip with fried eggplant and zucchini, raw veggies, or chips; also great on gyros and sandwiches or as a topping for fried fish and roasted meats.

4 cups plain yogurt (Sour cream can be substituted.)

2 cucumbers, seeded and grated

4 teaspoons olive oil

3 tablespoons white vinegar

3 cloves garlic, finely minced

2 tablespoons finely chopped dill

¼ teaspoon salt

Combine all ingredients in a bowl and refrigerate for at least 1 hour.

Yields 5 cups

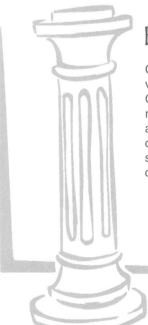

Big Fat Greek Fact

Cucumbers are one of the oldest cultivated vegetables and were eaten by ancient Greeks and Romans. Greek cooks don't really "cook" anything with cucumbers. They are eaten plain with salt, included in the classic Greek salad, and blended into dips such as this *tzatziki*, a garlicky yogurt-cucumber dip.

Yogurt-Dill-Mint Spread

Yogurt is important to Greek cuisine. It adds life and body to desserts, sauces and soups and provides a cooling contrast to fiery dishes. This spread is good with pita chips or on a sandwich. If served as a dip, garnish with a sprig of mint.

1 cucumber, peeled, seeded, and grated

2 cups plain yogurt

4 tablespoons finely chopped fresh mint

2 teaspoons finely chopped dill

1 teaspoon ground coriander

1 teaspoon granulated sugar

1 teaspoon salt

1 teaspoon white pepper

Mix all ingredients in a mixing bowl and refrigerate at least 1 hour. Serve cold.

Yields 4 cups

Big Fat Greek Fact

Greek yogurt, which is thicker and creamier then normal yogurt, is sometimes difficult to locate. If you can not find authentic Greek yogurt, try draining whole fat yogurt through cheesecloth for a few hours and then add honey and nuts.

Soups
and Salads

Greek Lemon Soup
"Avgolemono"

This is the traditional wedding soup in Greece. It is light and not too filling and is just the right soup to serve when having many courses.

4 cups chicken broth

2 cups water

3 lemons, freshly squeezed

½ tablespoon dill

½ teaspoon salt

⅛ teaspoon white pepper

5 large eggs, lightly beaten

1 cup hot cooked long-grain rice

1 cup boiled and diced chicken

Heat chicken broth and water in a saucepan. Add lemon juice, dill, salt, and pepper.

Place eggs in a large serving bowl. Stirring constantly, slowly add broth to the bowl with the egg mixture. Add rice and diced chicken.

Serve hot. Garnish with fresh parsley, if you like.

Serves 8

Big Fat Greek Fact

Since Greece has a year-round temperate climate, it has never really developed a soup tradition. Most Greek soups are simple to prepare. Vegetable, bean, and fish soups are the most popular. *Avgolemono* (a mixture of egg and lemon juice) gives many traditional soups a burst of flavor.

Lentil Soup
"Faki"

This soup hits the spot on a cold winter's day when all you want to do is bundle up in the covers on the couch. I like to add a little more red wine vinegar to my bowl to add just a little more punch.

½ cup olive oil

1 cup chopped onion

1 cup chopped carrot

1 cup chopped celery

3 cloves garlic, chopped fine

1 tablespoon oregano

2 bay leaves

1 cinnamon stick

1 cup tomato paste

1 pound lentils

2 quarts water

6 canned plum tomatoes, chopped, juice included

½ cup red wine vinegar

Salt and pepper to taste

Heat olive oil in soup pot over medium heat. Add onions, carrots, celery, garlic, oregano, bay leaves, and cinnamon stick. Sauté for about 5 minutes.

Add tomato paste and cook for 5 minutes, stirring constantly. Add lentils, water, and canned tomatoes and juice. Bring to boil and then reduce heat. Simmer until lentils are soft, about 30 to 45 minutes.

Season with vinegar, salt, and pepper. Serve hot.

Serves 6 to 8

Yankee Bean Soup
"Fasolada"

After all the years working in the restaurant business, my grandfather would make enough of this soup to feed 50 people. When he was done, not only would we eat it for a week but so would four of his friends' families.

1 pound white beans
½ cup olive oil
1 cup chopped onion
1 cup chopped carrot
1 cup chopped celery
3 cloves garlic, chopped fine
1 tablespoon oregano
2 bay leaves
1 cinnamon stick
1 cup tomato paste
2 quarts water
6 canned plum tomatoes, chopped, juice included
1 tablespoon thyme
Salt and pepper to taste

Rinse the beans, sorting out any broken or discolored ones. Soak overnight, then rinse well in fresh water. Reserve.

Heat olive oil in soup pot over medium heat. Add onions, carrots, celery, garlic, oregano, bay leaves, and cinnamon stick. Sauté for about 5 minutes.

Add tomato paste and cook for 5 minutes, stirring constantly. Add beans, water, and canned tomatoes and juice. Bring to boil and then reduce heat. Simmer until beans are soft, about 45 minutes.

Season with thyme, salt, and pepper.

Serves 6 to 8

Ouzo and Melon Soup

This is a great summertime soup. It is cool and refreshing. You can even add a teaspoon of dill to the honeydew mixture for a bigger contrast in flavor.

4 cups peeled and cubed honeydew melon

2 cups peeled and cubed cantaloupe

¼ cup ouzo

¼ cup firmly packed brown sugar

Place honeydew melon, 2 tablespoons ouzo, and 2 tablespoons brown sugar in a blender or food processor and process until smooth. Pour into 4 serving bowls and reserve.

Place cantaloupe and remaining 2 tablespoons ouzo and 2 tablespoons brown sugar in a blender or food processor and process until smooth. Gently scoop or pour cantaloupe mixture into the center of each bowl on top of the honeydew mixture.

Chill bowls in refrigerator. Serve cold and garnish with a sprig of mint.

Serves 4

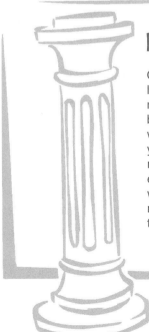

Big Fat Greek Fact

Ouzo is a clear, sweet, anise-flavored liqueur usually served as an apéritif. It is made from pressed grapes, herbs, and berries, including aniseed, licorice, mint, wintergreen, fennel, and hazelnut. In Greece you can sample ouzo at an *ouzeri*, a casual restaurant that serves *mezedes* or appetizers designed to match ouzo. A good *ouzeri* will have as many varieties of this Greek national drink as possible. Some offer more than 200 different brands!

Fennel, Feta, and Kalamata Olive Salad

Fennel has a very strong licorice flavor; but when you shred the bulb and add the other components of this recipe, the fennel serves as a sweet background flavor to an incredible salad.

1 (½ pound) fennel bulb

¼ cup lemon juice

1 tablespoon olive oil

¼ teaspoon sugar

⅛ teaspoon salt

⅛ teaspoon pepper

¼ cup pitted and chopped kalamata olives

4 ounces feta cheese, crumbled

Clean fennel well and remove outer layers and top stocks. (Top portion may be frozen to be used for flavoring at a later time.) Using a knife or mandolin, slice fennel into the thinnest shreds possible. Soak fennel in ice water for 30 minutes. Drain well.

In a bowl combine lemon juice, olive oil, sugar, salt, and pepper. Toss in shredded fennel. Top with chopped olives and crumbled feta cheese.

Serves 2 to 4

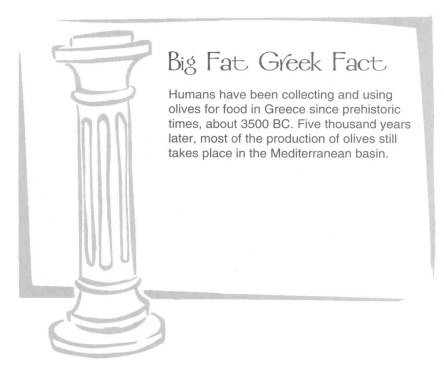

Big Fat Greek Fact

Humans have been collecting and using olives for food in Greece since prehistoric times, about 3500 BC. Five thousand years later, most of the production of olives still takes place in the Mediterranean basin.

Great Greek Bean Salad

You really can't go wrong with chickpeas and feta. This salad is hearty and bursting with fresh, contrasting flavors and textures. Serve it at your next BBQ or picnic, or just eat it right out of the refrigerator.

¼ pound string beans

1 (15.5 ounce) can chickpeas, drained and rinsed

1 (15.5 ounce) can kidney beans, drained and rinsed

½ red onion, chopped

1 cup pitted and chopped kalamata olives

¼ cup chopped parsley

1 cup crumbled feta cheese

½ cup lemon juice

2 tablespoons olive oil

2 cloves garlic, finely minced

1 tablespoon finely chopped fresh dill

1 tablespoon sugar

1 teaspoon each salt and pepper

Cook string beans in salted water until tender. Shock the beans by transferring them from the boiling water directly into ice water.

Drain string beans and place in a large bowl. Add chickpeas, kidney beans, red onion, olives, parsley, and feta and stir to combine.

In a small bowl mix together lemon juice, olive oil, garlic, dill, sugar, and salt and pepper. Pour mixture over beans and toss. Refrigerate and serve cold.

Serves 6 to 8

Greek Egg Salad
"Avgo Salata"

This is a classic dish that has a Greek kick to it. The yogurt and dill just add a new dimension to an American diner favorite.

8 hard-boiled eggs

¼ cup plain low-fat yogurt

1 tablespoon Dijon mustard

1 tablespoon each salt and pepper

1 tablespoon lemon juice

1 teaspoon finely chopped fresh dill

Slice up hard-boiled eggs and put in a bowl. Add all other ingredients and mix carefully so not to break up the egg slices too much.

Serve cold either alone, over salad greens, or on a sandwich.

Serves 2 to 4

Warm Zucchini Salad
"Kolokithakia Salata"

Substitution should be the name of this recipe. Instead of zucchini, use your favorite vegetable: whether it is asparagus, cauliflower, broccoli, or string beans, this recipe easily adapts.

2 pounds baby zucchini

½ cup lemon juice

1 cup olive oil

½ teaspoon each salt and pepper

Cut zucchini into ½-inch pieces. Boil until softened.

Mix lemon juice, olive oil, and salt and pepper in a small bowl. Pour mixture over zucchini and serve warm.

Serves 4 to 6

Greek-style Potato Salad
"Patatosalata"

This potato salad is spiked with capers which give it a bold, flavorful punch. Since it contains no mayonnaise, it can be served at a picnic or left out on a buffet for quite a while, and you don't need to worry about it spoiling.

1 pound potatoes, boiled, cooled, skinned, and cut into bite-size pieces

2 tomatoes, skinned and quartered

2 cucumbers, skinned and sliced

1 cup capers

½ cup chopped scallions

¼ cup chopped parsley

½ cup oil

½ cup vinegar

1 tablespoon each salt and pepper

Combine first 6 ingredients together in a large bowl.

Combine remaining ingredients in a separate bowl and whisk together. Pour over potato mixture and toss to combine.

Refrigerate and serve cold.

Serves 4 to 6

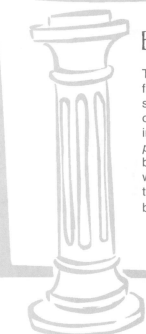

Big Fat Greek Fact

There are many boiled salads to choose from in Greek cuisine. Some have definite seasons, like boiled baby zucchini with olive oil and lemon dressing which is served only in the summer. Some, like potato salad — *patatosalata* — are year-round dishes because the potatoes are a blank canvas to which seasonal ingredients, such as capers, tomatoes, boiled eggs, and fresh herbs, can be added.

Greek Shrimp Salad

This is great for a summer gathering. I like to serve it over a bed of arugula along with Mediterranean Pita Chips.

1½ cups plain yogurt

2 tablespoons fresh lemon juice

¼ cup finely diced red onions

1 tablespoon finely diced cucumber

1 tablespoon finely chopped fresh dill

1 teaspoon sugar

8 ounces cooked baby shrimp, loosely chopped

Mix together all ingredients except shrimp. Add shrimp and fold to combine. Refrigerate and serve cold.

Serves 2

Greek Salad Dressing

You can use an electric mixer for easier emulsification. An emulsion is the mixture of two or more incompatible liquids. One is usually a fat or oil and the other is water-based. This is done by mixing the fats slowly into the liquids at a high speed until the liquids are suspended in each other.

1 cup lemon juice

¼ cup Dijon mustard

2 tablespoons minced garlic

1 tablespoon finely chopped fresh dill

1 tablespoon finely chopped fresh parsley

1 tablespoon finely chopped fresh oregano

2 teaspoons sugar

½ teaspoon kosher salt

2½ cups olive oil

In a mixing bowl whisk together all ingredients expect olive oil. After all ingredients are well mixed and there are no lumps, slow whisk in the oil until emulsified.

Refrigerate and use when needed.

Yields approximately 4 cups

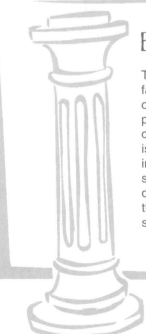

Big Fat Greek Fact

The Greek salad made Greek cuisine famous worldwide. Greeks call this mixture of tomatoes, cucumbers, onions, green peppers, olives, oregano, olive oil, and feta cheese *horiatiki*. The key to all Greek salads is freshness and seasonally appropriate ingredients. Good Greek cooks respect the seasons, so different salads are served during the spring, summer, and fall. During the winter, simple cabbage salads or boiled salads are standard.

Chicken, Meat, and Seafood Entrees

Chicken with Red Pepper Coulis
"Kotopoulo me Peperia Saltsa"

Red pepper coulis is a great thing to have in your refrigerator. It adds lots of flavor and color to any dish. By adding the red pepper flakes you turn the intensity way up.

4 boneless, skinless chicken breasts

1 tablespoon each salt and pepper

½ cup olive oil

1 cup Greek-style Red Pepper Coulis (Recipe appears on page 100.)

1 tablespoon red pepper flakes

Season chicken breasts with salt and pepper. Heat oil in a sauté pan. Add chicken and sauté chicken until cooked and browned on both sides.

Drain extra oil from pan. Add red pepper coulis and red pepper flakes and simmer until sauce is hot.

Plate and serve hot.

Yields 4 servings

Chicken Sautéed with Apples

"Kotopoulo me Mila"

Metaxa is a smooth and easy brandy from Greece. It comes in three grades. The lowest grade is fine for cooking, but the high grade version is preferred for drinking. What a pleasure — a small glass of Metaxa 7 Star at the end of an abundant meal.

4 boneless, skinless chicken breasts

1 tablespoon each salt and pepper

¼ cup flour

½ cup olive oil

2 apples, peeled and cubed

½ cup apple juice

1 shot Metaxa

1 teaspoon sugar

Season chicken with salt and pepper, then dredge in flour.

Heat oil in a sauté pan. Add chicken and sauté chicken until brown on one side. Turn and add apples. Continue to sauté until cooked through.

Drain extra oil from pan. Add apple juice, Metaxa, and sugar. Cook until liquid becomes a thin syrup.

Yields 4 servings

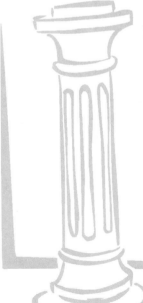

Big Fat Greek Fact

Apples have a long history. Prehistoric man ate wild apples, but they were only 1 to 2 inches in diameter and very acidic. Apple cultivation probably started with the beginning of agriculture in Europe. The Greek writer Theophrastus mentions a few varieties grown in Greece in the fourth century B.C. By the first century A.D., Pliny knew of 36 different kinds growing throughout Europe.

Stuffed Chicken Florentine

A savory union of spinach, sun-dried tomatoes, and feta all wrapped inside a tender, crispy chicken breast. This will be a new family favorite.

6 (6-ounce) boneless chicken breast halves with skin

½ cup seasoned breadcrumbs

4 cups torn spinach

½ cup crumbled feta cheese

¼ cup chopped sun-dried tomato halves

2 teaspoons melted butter

1 teaspoon chopped fresh dill

⅛ teaspoon pepper

2 teaspoons butter, softened

Preheat oven to 350°.

Place each chicken breast between 2 sheets of heavy-duty plastic wrap and flatten to ¼-inch thick. Dredge chicken in breadcrumbs and set aside to rest.

In a bowl mix spinach, feta, sun-dried tomatoes, melted butter, dill, and pepper. Divide mixture into 6 portions and spread evenly over each breast. Tuck in one side of the breast and roll so that the stuffing does not fall out of the chicken breasts. Place on a sheet pan. Top each breast with some softened butter.

Bake until center on chicken roll is cooked, about 35 minutes. (You might have to cover with foil half-way through cooking so the top doesn't burn.)

Yields 6 servings

Lemon Roasted Chicken
"Kotopoulo Lemonato"

Abundant lemon juice gives this recipe a gentle tang and a bright flavor.

1 whole chicken, cut into pieces
1 tablespoon each salt and pepper
1 cup flour
1 cup olive oil
1 pound potatoes, peeled and cubed
1 pound carrots, peeled and cubed
1 tablespoon chopped fresh dill
3 cups water
1 cup fresh lemon juice
1 cup white wine

Preheat oven to 350°.

Season chicken with salt and pepper and then dredge in flour. Heat oil in a roasting pan on stove top over medium-high heat. Sear chicken on both sides. Add remaining ingredients to pan and transfer to oven. Roast for 1½ hours or until chicken is cooked and potatoes are softened. (More water might be needed three-quarters of the way through the cooking process.)

Place on a platter and top with extra juice from roasting pan.

Yields 2 to 4 servings

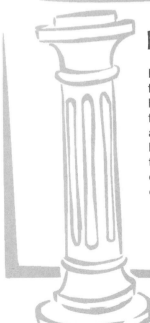

Big Fat Greek Fact

Even though hundreds of fresh herbs flourish in the wild, Greeks generally use dry herbs in the kitchen; only a few are used fresh. Dill is one of the exceptions. Fresh dill and lemons are essential to the Greek kitchen. There are a few flavor combinations that are unquestionably Greek: lemon and dill; lemon and olive oil; lemon, olive oil, oregano, and garlic; and lemon and eggs.

Baked Chicken in a Red Sauce
"Kotopoulo Kokinisto"

Nothing smells better than a chicken roasting in the oven. This is a very flavorful but simple recipe.

1 roasting chicken, split and cleaned

3 tablespoons butter, softened

2 tablespoons dried oregano

1 teaspoon each salt and pepper

4 cups Greek Tomato Sauce (Recipe appears on page 101.)

½ cup red wine

Preheat oven to 350°. Rub butter over entire chicken. Sprinkle with oregano and salt and pepper.

Heat an ovenproof frying pan on the stove over medium-high heat until hot. Place chicken, skin side down, in pan and sear. Turn and sear on the other side.

Cover chicken with Greek tomato sauce and red wine. Transfer to the oven. Bake for approximately 45 to 60 minutes or until chicken is fully cooked.

Yields 2 to 4 servings

Baked Chicken with Oregano
"Kotopoulo Oreganata"

This is a very simple dish — you'll see there aren't alot of ingredients — but the combination adds a great deal of subtle flavor and your kitchen will smell like heaven.

1 roasting chicken, split and cleaned

3 tablespoons butter, softened

2 tablespoons dried oregano

1 teaspoon each salt and pepper

½ cup white wine

4 tablespoons lemon juice

Preheat oven to 350°. Rub butter over entire chicken. Sprinkle with oregano and salt and pepper.

Heat an ovenproof frying pan on the stove over medium-high heat until hot. Place chicken, skin side down, in pan and sear. Turn and sear on the other side.

Cover chicken with white wine and lemon juice. Transfer to the oven. Bake for approximately 45 to 60 minutes or until chicken is fully cooked.

Yields 2 to 4 servings

Big Fat Greek Fact

Oregano grows wild all over the mountains of Greece. In fact, oregano in Greek means "joy of the mountains" or "mountain joy." This is because the oregano roots protect soil from washing away from the mountain when there is heavy rain. (I think it's also because the mountains just smell so good when oregano is blooming in the summer.)

Meat Kabobs
"Souvlakia"

This is a great summertime dish to make on the BBQ. I like to invite my closest friends and family to my house, and we eat the souvlakia hot from the grill. Bet you can't eat just one! A great tip: top the souvlakia with tzaziki sauce and serve in a toasted pita bread.

3 pounds lamb, beef, pork, or chicken, cubed

2 onions, quartered

2 green bell peppers, seeds removed, cut in 1-inch squares

2 tomatoes, cut in 1-inch squares

10 mushroom caps

3 tablespoons olive oil

2 tablespoons dried oregano

2 tablespoons each salt and pepper

3 lemons, quartered

Arrange meat on skewers, alternating meat with vegetables. Brush with olive oil and sprinkle with oregano, salt, and pepper.

Preheat the broiler or barbecue and grill for about 10 minutes, turning once or twice, until meat is the temperature that you like.

Squeeze lemon juice over the kabobs and serve hot.

Yields 6 to 8 kabobs

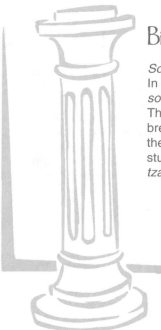

Big Fat Greek Fact

Souvlakia is the Greek national street food. In Greece there are restaurants called *souvlatzidikos* that specialize in *souvlakia*. They serve *souvlakia* either wrapped in pita bread (called *souvlakia*-pita) or straight from the skewer (*kalamaki*). *Souvlakia* are also stuffed into pitas with tomatoes, onions, *tzatziki*, and oftentimes, French fries.

Meatballs in Greek Tomato Sauce
"Soutzoukakia"

The Greek word *soutzoukaki* comes from the Turkish word *soujouk*, which is a type of dry sausage. The Greek "aki" ending means "*little one.*" So a *soutzoukaki* is literally *a little sausage*-looking meatball. I actually don't make mine sausage-shaped. I prefer them to be round, but you can make them anyway you like.

2 pounds ground beef

1 cup finely chopped onion

2 cloves garlic, minced

2 cups breadcrumbs, moistened (fresh white bread preferred)

2 eggs

2 tablespoons chopped parsley

½ tablespoon chopped mint

2 tablespoons each salt and pepper

1 teaspoon ground coriander

1 teaspoon cinnamon

Vegetable oil for frying

Greek Tomato Sauce (Recipe appears on page 101.)

Combine all ingredients, except vegetable oil and sauce, in a bowl. Use your hands to mix well. Roll into bite-size balls and dredge in flour. Fry balls in cooking oil until brown and cooked inside.

Add to a pot containing Greek tomato sauce and let simmer. Serve with rice or potatoes.

Yields 16 to 20 meatballs

Beef Stuffed Vegetables
"Yemista"

My wife loves when the "yemista" are mixed—when there are peppers and tomatoes together. I personally like to separate the vegetables that are going to be stuffed and bake them in individual casseroles. I make just peppers or just tomatoes because when I bake them together, I think the tomatoes end up tasting like peppers.

6 large tomatoes

6 bell peppers

½ cup olive oil

1 pound ground beef (Other meats can be used.)

2 cloves garlic, finely chopped

1 onion, finely chopped

1 cup uncooked short-grain rice

¼ cup finely chopped parsley

2 teaspoons tomato paste

1 teaspoon sugar

1 teaspoon each salt and pepper

Slice the tops off the tomatoes and peppers. Remove pulp from tomatoes, chop, and set aside. Scoop out the seeds from the peppers. Throw away seeds and reserve peppers.

Heat oil in a large sauté pan. Add ground beef, onion, and garlic and sauté until meat is browned. Add reserved chopped tomatoes, rice, parsley, tomato paste, sugar, salt, and pepper. Cook until everything is hot and well combined.

Preheat oven to 350°. Fill each vegetable with some stuffing and place in a casserole dish. Fill the casserole dish with enough water to cover the vegetables half-way up. Cover. Bake for approximately 1½ hours until rice is tender. (You may need to add more water.) Serve warm or at room temperature.

Serves 6 to 12

Roast Leg of Lamb

At Easter time or *Pascha* it is traditional for a Greek family to eat lamb. The best experience for a traditional *Pascha* is to cook the entire baby lamb on the spit for hours in the backyard.

2 heads garlic, minced or pressed

2 cups lemon juice

1 cup Dijon mustard

1 (8 pound) leg of lamb

3 tablespoons oregano

Kosher salt and pepper

2 carrots, chopped roughly

2 celery ribs, chopped

1 onion, chopped

3 cups red wine

2 rosemary sprigs

1 tablespoon Roux (Recipe appears on page 103.)

Place pressed garlic in a mortar and pestle and grind garlic into a mush. (You can also process in a food processor.) Transfer garlic to a bowl. Add lemon juice and mustard and mix well.

Trim lamb of extra fat and place in bottom of roasting pan. Cover the outside of the lamb with oregano, salt, and pepper and then rub lamb with garlic mixture.

Preheat oven to 350°. Add carrots, celery, and onions to pan. Roast for about 1½ hours or until meat reaches desired temperature.

Remove lamb from roasting pan. Allow to rest 15 minutes before carving.

Add wine to pan to deglaze. Stir to remove bits of browned meat from the bottom of the pan. Strain juices and drippings into a saucepan. Heat over medium heat. Add rosemary. Add roux to sauce and whisk until sauce thickens.

Carve lamb and serve with sauce on the side. Serve with Greek Vegetables or Roasted Vegetables (Recipes appear on page 79 and page 80.).

Serves 12 to 15

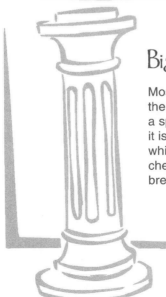

Big Fat Greek Fact

Most people are familiar with the image of the Greek Easter feast with a whole lamb on a spit. Although lamb is traditionally served, it is just one element of the Easter menu which would also include offal, fresh spring cheeses, artichokes, eggs, and specialty breads and cookies.

Baked Orzo with Lamb
"Giouvetsi me Arni"

Every Greek has someone in the family who makes the best giouvesti, so join the club. Change this around, add your favorite little something, and make this recipe your family's own special giouvesti.

2 pounds lamb, cubed

½ cup olive oil

4 cloves garlic, chopped

1 shallot, chopped fine

1 pound orzo

4 cups chopped canned
   tomatoes

3 cups water

2 teaspoons tomato paste

¼ cup Parmesan cheese

1 teaspoon oregano

1 teaspoon sugar

1 bay leaf

Preheat oven to 350°. Sear cubed lamb in a large oven-ready pot. Add olive oil, garlic, and shallots and sauté.

Wash orzo with warm water and add it to the pot. Add all remaining ingredients. Bake 60 minutes until pasta is cooked.

Serves 6 to 8

Greek Burger

I like to call this "endless possibilities." Why? You can serve it in a number of styles: either in a pita pocket topped with bean sprouts, sliced tomatoes, and tzaziki sauce; or on a plate with a little squeeze of fresh lemon juice.

2 pounds ground lamb

2 cloves garlic, chopped

1 shallot, chopped fine

½ cup feta cheese

¼ cup pitted and chopped kalamata olive

1 teaspoon oregano

Mix all ingredients together. Form mixture into 6 burgers.

Grill until desired doneness.

Serve in pita pockets with your choice of toppings.

Serves 6

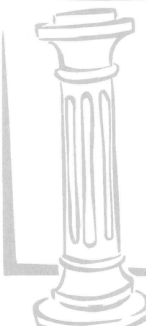

Big Fat Greek Fact

Greeks are the largest consumers of red meat in the European Union. That's pretty amazing considering that until just a generation ago, meat, a luxury, was usually served just a few times a month and on holidays. Ground meat — *kimas* in Greek — is prepared many ways. Two regions have special meat dishes. In Kefalonia you'll find a meat pie that is made of ground pork, lamb, and veal; and during the Christmas season in Ipiros, you can sample a festive ground meat pie baked with béchamel sauce.

Pork Chops in a Wine Sauce
"Brízoles Hirínes"

If you don't have a lot of time to stand in front of a stove cooking for hours, yet you want that impression in an entree, this is the dish for you. All that is needed is a little prep work, then toss it in the oven. By the time you're finished getting the table and veggies ready, the pork chops will be done.

12 pork chops, about 1-inch thick

1 tablespoon oregano

1 tablespoon each salt and pepper

3 tablespoons olive oil

3 cloves garlic, minced

1 shallot, chopped

½ cup water

½ cup white wine

Preheat oven to 325°.

Season pork chops with oregano, salt, and pepper.

Heat a roasting pan on the stove over medium-high heat. Add pork chops and sear on each side. Add olive oil, garlic, and shallots and sauté for 3 minutes. Add water and white wine and bring to boil.

Transfer roasting pan to oven and braise until juices are evaporated and pork is cooked, about 20 to 30 minutes. Plate and serve.

Serves 6

Grilled Veal Chops
"Brizoles sti Skara"

Picture this...summertime is here, sitting outside on a sunny afternoon, and you're hungry. Just spark up the BBQ or a gas grill and you're ready to go. Fast and flavorful. For a variation, use baby lamb chops, but be prepared: in my family we eat them like lollypops. They just go right down and you can't stop.

12 veal chops, about ½-inch thick

2 tablespoons olive oil

2 tablespoons dried oregano

2 tablespoons each salt and pepper

2 lemons

Brush veal chops with olive oil and sprinkle with the oregano, salt, and pepper.

Place veal chops on grill. Baste occasionally with olive oil. Cook the veal to desired temperate.

Squeeze lemons over the veal chops and serve.

Serves 6

Big Fat Greek Fact

Meat is an important part of Greek holiday celebrations. During Carnival, the festive period before Lent, Greeks attend masked balls and indulge in eating plenty of meat and milk products. Meat is integral to this celebration: the word in Greek for Carnival is *apokries*, which means "of meat." The second week of Carnival is the meat-eating week. The Thursday of that week is called "sputtering" Thursday because of the sizzling sound meat makes when it hits a hot grill.

Fried Cod
"Bakaliaro"

The first time I ate this dish I was 16 years old. I was sitting in a little restaurant in the "Yialo" overlooking the bright blue Aegean Sea.

2 pounds dried cod

1½ cups all-purpose flour

1 cup beer (Water can be substituted.)

½ teaspoon pepper

½ teaspoon granulated garlic

½ lemon, juice only

½ teaspoon baking powder

Vegetable oil for frying

Cut cod into even sections depending on how many portions you would like. Cover with water and soak overnight. The next day, discard water.

Boil cod in water until half-way cooked. (This will make removing skin and bones easier). Remove skin and bones. Set aside and let cool.

Combine remaining ingredients, except vegetable oil, in a mixing bowl to make a batter. Dip cod in batter.

Heat oil in a heavy skillet over medium-high heat. Fry cod until golden brown on each side and cooked throughout.

Serve with lemon or with a dip such as Yogurt-Dill-Mint Spread (Recipe appears on page 31.) or Garlic Spread (Recipe appears on page 28.).

Serves 4

Big Fat Greek Fact

If you are looking for great fish in Greece, head to a *psarotaverna* (fish tavern). Most *psarotavernas* are located very close to the sea or a port. They are known for fresh whole grilled fish and seafood dishes. Fish is usually sold by the pound, and guests are welcome to walk into the kitchen and choose their own fish.

Grilled Red Snapper Oreganata

In Greece, most of the fish is prepared and served whole. This is good if you're not squeamish because when a fish is cooked whole, the juices are maintained, and the fish is incredibly moist. Also some of the best meat is found in the parts that are usually thrown out. However, if you do cut the head and fins off your fish, don't throw them out. Use them to make a fish stock by simmering the pieces in water with celery, onions, carrots, and lemons. This will make a great base for a soup or sauce.

1 whole red snapper
1 lemon, sliced
½ bunch oregano sprigs
2 tablespoons finely chopped fresh dill
¼ cup plus ½ cup olive oil
½ teaspoon black pepper
1 cup diced tomatoes
1 clove garlic, minced
3 tablespoons lemon juice

Heat grill until hot. Make diamond-shaped slits on each side of fish with a knife.

Place lemon, oregano, and dill into all cavities of the fish. Rub with ¼ cup olive oil and place on grill.

Grill for 8 minutes or until golden brown on each side, turning carefully.

Mix ½ cup olive oil, black pepper, tomatoes, garlic, and lemon juice together in a small mixing bowl.

Plate snapper and top with tomato mixture.

Serves 1 or 2

Mussels in Wine

"Midia Ahnista me Krassi"

Simple yet classy. Serve this over linguini and enjoy. If you don't like mussels, use clams or oysters—they both work great too.

2 tablespoons butter

3 cloves garlic, minced

1 shallot, minced

1 pound mussels, whole, beard removed and cleaned

1 cup white wine

1 teaspoon chopped fresh dill

Place butter, garlic, and shallots in a small pot. Sauté for 2 minutes. Add remaining ingredients and cover.

Cook until mussels open. (Remember to stir occasionally so garlic and shallots don't burn.)

Serves 1 to 2 as an entree
4 to 6 as an appetizer

Fried Squid
"Kalamari Tiganita"

It doesn't matter where in the Mediterranean you are from—everyone knows this dish. In Greece this dish is served with fresh lemon juice and no sauce. This is done because the fresh squid from the Mediterranean has such an amazing flavor you don't want to complicate it.

1 pound squid, beak and ink sac removed

2 tablespoons baking soda

1 cup Greek Tomato Sauce (Recipe appears on page 101.)

1 teaspoon crushed red pepper

1 teaspoon each salt and pepper

2 cups flour

Vegetable oil for frying

1 lemon

Cut squid into rings. Cut tentacles into ½-inch-long pieces. Sprinkle squid with baking soda and refrigerate for 30 minutes. (This will help to tenderize the squid.)

Combine tomato sauce and red pepper and heat through. Reserve.

Remove squid from refrigerator. Rinse under cold water and dry. Sprinkle squid with salt and pepper and dredge in flour. Heat oil in a medium-size frying pan over high heat. Fry squid in oil until golden brown. Remove from oil and place over a paper towel to drain.

Squeeze lemon over squid and serve with sauce. Serve immediately or squid will become tough.

Serves 4 as an appetizer
Serves 2 as an entree

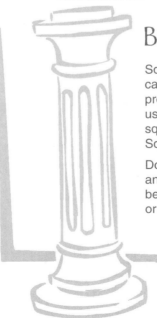

Big Fat Greek Fact

Squid, octopus, and shellfish are favorite catches from Greek waters and play a prominent role in the Greek diet. Squid is usually fried, grilled, or stewed. Very large squid are grilled whole, or stuffed and grilled. Squid is also frequently added to a stew pot.

Don't be scared of squid! This dish is simple and elegant; yet if not prepared properly, it can be a disaster. Don't skip the baking soda step, or the squid will become tough and rubbery.

Pasta and Vegetarian Entrees

Sea Scallops and Cherry Tomatoes over Shell Pasta

Here's a great way to add a little extra flavor and texture to this dish. Serve pasta in a bowl topped with baked Parmesan. To make baked Parmesan, coarsely grate Parmesan cheese and scatter over a baking sheet lined with parchment paper. Place in a 350° oven until cheese melts. Let cool and then break into pieces.

8 ounces uncooked shell pasta

1 tablespoon plus 1 teaspoon olive oil

½ cup chopped fresh parsley

5 cloves garlic, minced

1 teaspoon dried whole basil

½ teaspoon dried whole oregano

½ teaspoon salt

1 tablespoon all-purpose flour

¼ teaspoon pepper

8 ounces water

1¼ pounds sea scallops, cut into ½-inch pieces

15 cherry tomatoes, quartered

Cook pasta according to package directions or personal preference. Drain and rinse under cold running water. Set aside in a large bowl.

Heat 1 tablespoon oil in a pan. Add half the parsley, garlic, dried basil, dried oregano, and salt. Sauté until garlic is a golden color. (Be careful not to burn dry spices.) Add flour and pepper to the mixture, mixing constantly with a whisk. Gradually add water and stir until mixture thickens and there are no lumps. Pour sauce over pasta; set aside and keep warm.

Wipe pan clean. Heat remaining oil in the pan. When oil is hot, add scallops and cherry tomatoes. Sauté until scallops are cooked. Add to pasta mixture and toss gently with remaining parsley.

Serves 4

Greek Shrimp Ziti

For a great seafood ziti, follow this recipe then add scallops and crabmeat at the same stage as the shrimp.

1 tablespoon olive oil

1 pound medium shrimp, peeled and deveined

¾ pound ziti pasta, cooked and drained according to package

3 cups Greek Tomato Sauce (Recipe appears on page 101.)

2 cups diced plum tomatoes

¼ cup chopped parsley

2 teaspoons oregano

1 teaspoon red pepper flakes

2 cups crumbled feta cheese

Preheat oven to 400°.

Heat oil in an ovenproof skillet pan over medium-high heat. Add shrimp and sauté about 2 minutes until shrimp start to turn pink.

Remove shrimp from pan and chop. Combine shrimp and remaining ingredients in a large bowl.

Coat a baking pan with butter. Transfer mixture to pan and bake until cheese is softened and begins to melt, about 20 to 30 minutes. (Feta usually doesn't melt completely.) Serve hot.

Serves 4 to 6

Big Fat Greek Fact

Shrimp and mussels are the most favored shellfish in Greece. Very popular is the large *gambari* shrimp which is indigenous to the waters off the northwest coast of Greece. It is usually served grilled or fried. Often shrimp are fried whole and served shells and all. Mussels are often stuffed or fried. Mediterranean langoustine is best when prepared very simply, either steamed or boiled. In *tavernas* your langoustine will be accompanied by a superb olive oil and lemon dressing.

Greek-style Shrimp Scampi

Serve this over a large portion of capellini and make sure you have plenty of bread because you won't want to waste a drop of the juice.

1 teaspoon olive oil

1 pound large shrimp, peeled and deveined

6 cloves garlic, minced

3 tablespoons red wine

2 tomatoes, skinned and diced

1 cup crumbled feta cheese

¼ cup chopped parsley

¼ cup pitted and chopped kalamata olives

¼ teaspoon fresh ground pepper

Preheat oven to 350°.

Heat oil in an ovenproof skillet pan over medium-high heat. Add shrimp and garlic and sauté until shrimp start to turn pink. Add remaining ingredients.

Transfer skillet to oven and cook until shrimp are fully cooked, about 10 minutes.

Serves 2 to 4

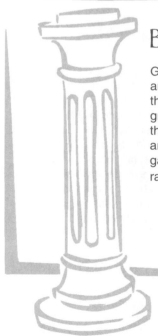

Big Fat Greek Fact

Garlic is essential to many classic sauces and dips. Can you imagine *tzatziki* without the bite of fresh garlic? Nuts and garlic go great together, and there are several sauces that combine walnuts and garlic or almonds and garlic. In spring, tender stalks of fresh garlic arrive at markets, and these are eaten raw with *taramosalata* dip.

Pastitsio

Pastitsio is a simple yet filling dish. Similar to lasagna, this is a staple at my house during the holidays or for family gatherings. It is one of those dishes that everyone seems to eat and enjoy.

2 pounds ziti pasta, cooked

1 quart Kima Sauce (Recipe appears on page 102.)

1 quart Krema (Recipe appears on page 103.)

1 cup grated Parmesan cheese

Cook pasta according to package directions or personal preference. Drain and rinse under cold running water. Reserve.

Preheat oven to 350°. Spread a thin layer of kima sauce along the bottom of a large baking dish. Top with half the cooked ziti. Pour remaining kima sauce over ziti. Top with enough kreama to cover all the pasta and to come to the top of the dish. Sprinkle with Parmesan cheese and bake for approximately 1 hour or until the kreama becomes a light golden brown.

Serves 12

Athenian Capellini

This dish is a favorite at the restaurant. The nice fresh ingredients bring the summer back to even the coldest day in winter. This dish reminds me of the time that my wife and I visited a little town in Santorini called Oia, where we ate dinner and saw the most incredible sunset.

2 tablespoons olive oil

1 cup chopped sweet onion

¼ cup capers

¼ cup pitted and chopped kalamata olive

2 cloves garlic, minced

2 teaspoons dried oregano

2 cups diced tomato

2 cups crumbled feta cheese

¼ cup chopped parsley

6 cups cooked capellini pasta

Heat oil in a large skillet. Add onions, capers, kalamata olives, garlic, and oregano and sauté until onions are softened and transparent. Toss in tomato and feta cheese and heat for 1 minute. Mix in parsley and serve over capellini.

Serves 2 to 4

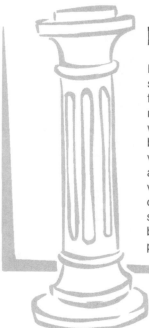

Big Fat Greek Fact

Necessity has given us a slew of Greek stews and stovetop meat recipes. Up until a few decades ago, many home kitchens did not have an indoor oven. The outdoor oven was difficult to use and reserved for only bread baking and holiday meals. Meat was very expensive, so it was used sparingly and combined with other ingredients like vegetables, beans, and rice. These casseroles — whether baked or prepared stovetop —are still appreciated today because they are inexpensive and easy to prepare.

Roasted Portabella-Pepper-Feta-Basil on Focaccia

You can use any thick crusted bread that you prefer. Just slice down. You can also toast the bread if you like a hot, crispy sandwich.

8 portabella mushrooms

2 teaspoons A-1® Steak Sauce

3 teaspoons Worcestershire sauce

8 slices focaccia bread

1 cup julienned roasted red peppers

8 fresh basil leaves, shredded

1 tomato, sliced

2 cups crumbled feta cheese

Lay out portabella mushrooms on a sheet pan and top with A-1 sauce and Worcestershire sauce. Bake until mushrooms are soft.

Lay bread out on a clean sheet pan. Top each slice with a portabella mushroom and then a layer of roasted peppers, basil leaves, sliced tomato, and finally with feta cheese.

Broil until cheese melts.

Serves 4 to 8

Feta Stuffed Peppers

"Piperies Yemistes me Feta"

Serve these stuffed beauties as an hors d'oeurve, first course, entree, or side dish.

¼ **pound cream cheese, softened**

¼ **pound feta cheese, crumbled**

½ **cup chopped parsley**

2 **tablespoons chopped dill**

8 **long mild green peppers, seeded**

2 **eggs, beaten**

4 **cups flour for dredging**

Vegetable oil for frying

Cream the cream cheese with an electric mixer. Add feta, parsley, and dill and cream until soft. Place mixture into a pastry bag and pipe cheese mixture into peppers.

Dip stuffed peppers into beaten egg and dredge in flour.

Heat oil over medium-high heat. Fry peppers until golden brown. Remove and drain on paper towel. Serve hot.

Yields 8 peppers

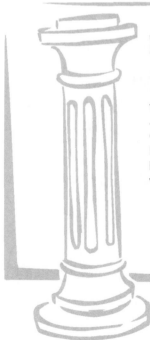

Big Fat Greek Fact

Greek stuffed peppers are called *yemisti*. Usually it is summer vegetables — peppers, tomatoes, zucchini, and eggplants — which are stuffed. The stuffing ingredients vary. Classic combinations are: rice, onions, and herbs; *trahana* (a milk-based tiny pasta); bulgur; ground meat, such as lamb or beef, with rice; or vegetables and herbs.

Mousaka

This is a traditional dish as well as one of the most well-known Greek dishes around. It has a unique flavor and is very easy to make.

5 pounds eggplant, cut into
  ¼-inch slices
Vegetable oil for cooking
5 pounds potato, cut into
  ¼-inch slices
1 quart Kima Sauce (Recipe
  appears on page 102.)
1 quart Krema (Recipe
  appears on page 103.)
1 cup grated Parmesan
  cheese

Preheat oven to 350°.

Lay sliced eggplant in a baking sheet and bake until eggplant softens, about 10 minutes.

Heat oil in a large skillet. Blanch sliced potatoes in oil until potatoes soften, about 5 minutes.

Spread a thin layer of kima sauce over the bottom of a 2-inch deep hotel pan or similar baking pan. Layer potato slices over sauce. Spread remaining kima sauce over potato slices. Layer eggplant over sauce.

Top with krema, spreading it evenly to the top of the baking dish. Sprinkle with Parmesan cheese. Bake for 1 hour or until the top is light golden brown.

Serves 12

Side Dishes

Beets and Greens with Garlic Sauce

"Patzaria me Skordalia"

I think beets are an underrated root vegetable. There is a huge amount of flavor in beets, and they are so versatile. They can be prepared just like potatoes. They can be mashed, baked, boiled, and fried. The leaves of the beets are hiding the majority of the nutrition so don't let them go to waste.

1 pound fresh beets

1 cup red wine vinegar

1 cup prepared Garlic Spread (Recipe appears on page 28.)

Remove stems and leaves from beets. Discard stems. Wash leaves well and reserve. Remove outer skin from beets. Quarter or slice beets.

Bring a large pot of water to boil. Add vinegar. Boil beets until they are fork tender, about 10 to 30 minutes depending on how thinly you cut them.

Remove beets from water. Add leaves from beets to boiling water and cook until tender, about 1 minute.

Arrange on a plate with leaves in center and beets surrounding leaves. Serve hot or cold with garlic spread (sauce).

Serves 6 to 8

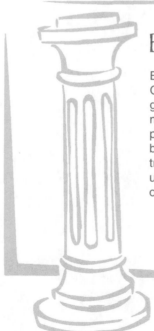

Big Fat Greek Fact

Boiled greens are an important part of the Greek cuisine. Chard, spinach, collard greens, dandelion greens, beet greens, and mustard greens are among the most popular. They all get prepared in the same basic way. First the greens are cleaned and trimmed, then boiled in lightly salted water until tender. The greens are seasoned with olive oil and either vinegar or lemon juice.

Baked String Beans in a Red Sauce

"Fasolakia Kokinista"

This recipe has so many variations. At the diner we make this with zucchini, string beans, eggplant, and even a mixture of them all. See what you can come up with — just be creative.

1 cup olive oil

1 onion, chopped fine

4 cloves garlic, chopped fine

2 pounds frozen string beans

2 cups diced tomato

½ cup water

2 tablespoons tomato paste

1 tablespoon chopped fresh dill

½ teaspoon sugar

½ teaspoon each salt and pepper

1 cinnamon stick

2 bay leaves

Preheat oven to 350°. Heat oil in a large ovenproof pot. Add onion and garlic and sauté. Add all other ingredients and simmer.

Bake, stirring occasionally, for 20 minutes or until string beans are soft. Serve hot.

Serves 6 to 8

Zucchini Souffle

Fresh vegetables are very important in Greek cuisine. Zucchini, spinach, and eggplant are the most frequently utilized. While this dish is made of some very classic Greek ingredients, it would be at home on a French menu as well.

2 teaspoons butter

1 pound zucchini, grated

2 eggs

1 cup milk

¼ cup finely chopped fresh dill

½ pound feta cheese

1 9-inch pie crust

Preheat oven to 350°. Melt butter in a frying pan over medium heat. Add grated zucchini and sauté until tender. Remove from heat.

In a bowl mix eggs, milk, and dill. Stir in feta and zucchini. Spoon mixture into pie crust.

Bake 30 to 45 minutes or until mixture thickens and a toothpick can be inserted and comes out dry. Serve hot.

Serves 4 to 6

Big Fat Greek Fact

In Greece, feta usually accompanies most meals, and pairs especially well with beans, rice, poultry, and lamb. Try serving feta sprinkled with oregano and drizzled with olive oil as the first course of a meal.

Greek Vegetables

Bring bold colors and exciting flavors to your dinner table with this healthy dish. Serve reheated leftovers stuffed into a pita or sandwich roll. Even better, top with your choice of cheese and brown under the broiler.

¼ cup olive oil

2 cloves garlic, minced

1 onion, sliced thin

12 cherry tomatoes, halved

4 mushrooms, quartered

2 small canned artichoke hearts, quartered

½ each red and green bell pepper, trimmed, seeded, and sliced

¼ fennel bulb, sliced thin

½ cup white wine

Salt and pepper to taste

Heat olive oil in a sauté pan over medium-hot heat. Add garlic and onion and sauté until transparent. Add remaining ingredients and simmer until liquid reduces and vegetables are soft.

Season to taste with salt and pepper.

Serves 4 to 6

Roasted Vegetables

Roasting gives vegetables a sweet, rich flavor. The sweetness happens because the roasting process drives out water and the natural sugars in the vegetables caramelize. It's a low-fat, healthy way to prepare almost any vegetable, including bell peppers, turnips, squash, tomatoes, mushrooms, brussel sprouts, sweet potatoes, beets, and eggplant.

½ **pound red bliss potatoes, quartered**

½ **pound carrots, diced**

3 red onions, diced

4 cloves garlic, chopped

2 cups lemon juice

1 cup chicken broth or water

2 tablespoons dried oregano

Preheat oven to 350°.

Toss all ingredients together and place in a roasting pan. Roast vegetables in oven about 35 to 45 minutes until fork tender, stirring occasionally.

Serves 4 to 6

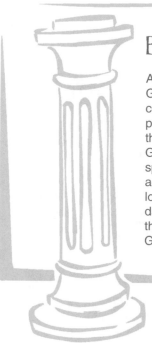

Big Fat Greek Fact

According to legend, potatoes came to Greece in the 1820s during the tenure of the country's first prime minister. He was a smart politician and understood that even though there was nutritional value in the potatoes, the Greek citizens would reject anything state sponsored. In order to make them more acceptable, he ordered that the potatoes be locked overnight in the capital city. The next day — as he predicted — it was discovered that the spuds had been stolen, and the Greeks love affair with potatoes began.

Grecian Stuffed Potatoes

Twice baked potatoes aren't just plain anymore. Just try this recipe and you'll love it like I do. This is also something fancy to do if you are trying to impress someone with your cooking. You can prepare them ahead of time and broil them just before serving. Remember, for an elegant look, pipe the stuffing back into the potato with a pastry bag.

4 baking potatoes

1 tablespoon olive oil

4 ounces artichoke hearts, chopped

½ cup finely chopped onion

3 tablespoons minced kalamata olives

2 cloves garlic, minced

½ teaspoon dried oregano

½ cup milk

¼ cup butter

1 cup crumbled feta cheese

1 cup diced tomato

1 teaspoon chopped fresh dill

Preheat oven to 425°. Wash potatoes. Poke a few times with a fork, then wrap in foil. Bake for 45 to 55 minutes or until tender.

Remove potatoes from foil and cut in half. Use a spoon to scoop out insides and place in a large mixing bowl. Save skins.

Heat olive oil in a skillet. Add artichoke hearts, onions, kalamata olives, garlic, and oregano. Add mixture to the potatoes. Add milk and butter and mash all ingredients together until they are smooth. (An electric mixer can be used.) When smooth, fold in feta, tomato, and dill.

With a spoon stuff the potato mixture back into the potato skins. (For a more decorative look, use a pastry bag and tip.)

Place under the broiler or bake until the tops become golden brown.

Serves 8

Pilafi

This dish goes back to the days when cooks would put all the ingredients in a single big pot and let simmer all day. Thankfully, you only have to let it simmer 30 minutes.

2 cups long-grain converted rice
4 cups chicken broth
2 bouillon cubes
1 teaspoon butter
1 teaspoon salt
1 teaspoon pepper
1 lemon, halved
1 bay leaf

Wash rice well to remove starch and prevent rice from sticking.

Combine all ingredients in a pot over medium heat. Simmer, stirring occasionally to prevent the rice from sticking to the bottom of the pot, until all the chicken broth is gone and the rice is cooked, about 20 to 30 minutes.

Remove lemon halves and bay leaf before serving.

Serves 6 to 8

Spinach and Rice
"Spanakorizo"

My father told me that when he was growing up in Andros, a small island off the main peninsula of Greece, he would practically live off this dish because it was very inexpensive to make.

1 cup short-grain rice
½ cup olive oil
5 scallions, finely chopped
3 cloves garlic
1 pound frozen spinach, defrosted and chopped
3 tablespoons chopped fresh dill
2 lemons, juice only

Cook rice according to package instructions and reserve.

Heat oil in a skillet. Add scallions and garlic and sauté for 5 minutes. Add cooked rice, spinach, dill, and lemon juice.

Stir until mixture becomes hot.

Serves 4 as an entree
Serves 12 as a side dish

Big Fat Greek Fact

Buy loose spinach rather than packaged. Make sure the leaves are fresh, firm, and dark green, without insect holes, blackened decay spots, or yellow edges. If you detect a sour smell, it's past its prime. To properly clean spinach, remove the tough stems. Fill a stockpot with tap water and add spinach. Swirl it around to loosen dirt and then strain in a colander.

Greek Couscous

Couscous is used all over the world. Some say it is a pasta and others, a grain. Actually it is the separated grain of the wheat plant which is dried and milled and becomes semolina flour used primarily to make pasta. Couscous is also a North African grain cooked in a large kettle with a steamer on top in which bulgur wheat is cooked as a side dish.

1½ cups water

1 cup uncooked couscous

¼ teaspoon salt

3 tablespoons lemon juice

2 teaspoons chopped fresh dill

¼ teaspoon ground pepper

1½ tablespoons extra-virgin olive oil

2 cups cherry tomatoes, quartered

⅓ cup crumbled feta cheese

¼ cup pitted and chopped kalamata olives

¼ cup chopped red onion

Bring water to a boil in a medium saucepan Add couscous and salt and stir. Remove from heat; cover and let stand 5 minutes. Fluff with a fork. (Check to make sure this corresponds with directions on box. Your couscous may vary.)

Combine lemon juice, dill, and pepper in a mixing bowl. While mixing rapidly, add the oil in a slow steady stream. This will make a creamy dressing.

Add tomatoes, feta, olives, and red onions to the dressing. Stir dressing into couscous. Serve warm or hot.

Serves 4

Mediterranean Risotto

A new twist on a traditional Italian specialty. Risotto is a creamy Italian dish made with short-grained rice, butter, onions, and hot stock. Remember to add the stock in stages for a nice velvety dish.

2 teaspoons vegetable oil

2 cups chopped sweet onion

3 cloves garlic, minced

2 cups Arborio rice, uncooked

18 ounces chicken stock

1 cup crumbled feta cheese

⅓ cup chopped parsley

¼ cup grated Parmesan cheese

¼ cup pitted and chopped kalamata olive

Pepper to taste

Heat oil in a saucepot. Add onion and garlic and sauté until onion is transparent. Stir in rice.

Add half the stock and stir constantly until all stock is absorbed. Repeat this step with the remaining stock.

Remove rice from stove. Stir in remaining ingredients and plate in a decorative bowl.

Serves 6

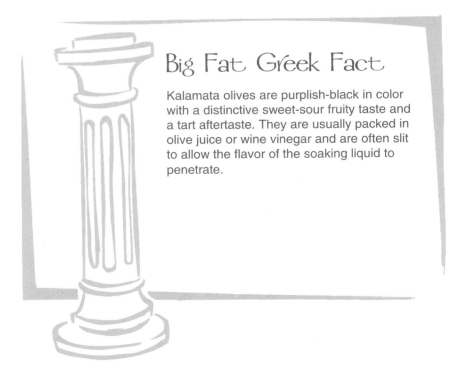

Big Fat Greek Fact

Kalamata olives are purplish-black in color with a distinctive sweet-sour fruity taste and a tart aftertaste. They are usually packed in olive juice or wine vinegar and are often slit to allow the flavor of the soaking liquid to penetrate.

Desserts

Almond Cookies

Almond cookies are found throughout the world in every cuisine. In some parts they are hard cookies and others are soft patties. I found both are equally enjoyed. I like to serve these on a plate with vanilla ice cream and sprinkle them with cinnamon and powdered sugar.

1 cup blanched almonds

1⅓ cups sugar

1¼ cups all-purpose flour

¼ teaspoon baking powder

3 egg whites

1 teaspoon amaretto

1 teaspoon Metaxa

1 teaspoon rose water (optional)

Preheat oven to 350°.

Place almonds in a food processor and pulse until finely ground. Add sugar, flour, and baking powder to almonds and blend well. Add remaining ingredients and mix until wet and dry are evenly distributed. (This will be a thick mixture.)

With wet hands roll mixture into 30 balls and place on a baking sheet with parchment paper.

Bake for 25 minutes or until crisp on the outside and soft on the inside. Cool before eating.

Yields approximately 30 cookies

Almond Macaroons
"Amygdalota"

Amygdalota is the Greek equivalent to the macaroon. In some areas of Greece, like the island that my wife is from, the macaroons are hard on the outside and soft in the middle. However, on the island that my family is from, the macaroons are soft inside and out.

2 pounds almond paste
1 pound confectioners' sugar
¼ cup rosewater
6 egg whites

Preheat oven to 350°. Fit 2 baking sheets with parchment paper.

Mix almond paste and confectioners' sugar in an electric mixer fitted with a paddle. Add rose water. Slowly add egg whites until mixture is loose enough to pipe out a pastry bag but not soupy.

Put mixture into pastry bag and form into small round cookies on parchment paper.

Bake for approximately 20 minutes or until golden brown.

Yields approximately 12 cookies

Big Fat Greek Fact

Almond paste, found in most supermarkets, is made of blanched, ground almonds combined with sugar. Ground peaches or apricots are often added to enhance the flavor of the almond. After opening, wrap tightly and refrigerate so that the almond paste does not get dried out. If it does get dry, just heat in a microwave for a few seconds.

Greek Butter Cookie
"Koulourakia"

Koulourakias are made in every Greek home at Easter. Traditionally they are coated with sesame seeds. But I (and everyone I know) always scrape off the seeds; so my koulourakias are always seedless.

- ¾ **pound butter**
- 1½ **cups sugar**
- 2 **eggs**
- 2 **tablespoons Metaxa (Greek cognac)**
- 2 **tablespoons vanilla extract**
- 5 **cups flour**
- 1½ **teaspoons baking powder**
- ¾ **teaspoon baking soda**
- 1 **egg, beaten**

Preheat oven to 350°. Fit baking sheets with parchment paper.

Cream together butter and sugar in an electric mixer. With mixer running, slowly add 2 eggs, Metaxa, and vanilla. Slowly add flour, baking powder, and baking soda and blend just until the dough comes together.

Remove from bowl and knead with your hands. On a floured board roll tablespoon-size pieces into ropes. Cookies can be formed into whatever shape you prefer. (I like to braid mine or twist two small pieces together to form a short rope. Other shapes are balls with flattened bottoms or S-shapes.)

Place on parchment lined tray and brush with beaten egg. Bake until golden in color, about 30 to 45 minutes.

Yields approximately 20 cookies
(depending on how you shape them)

Big Fat Greek Fact

Greeks love their cookies. Among the favorites are *voutimata* and *paximadia* which are not too sweet and eaten with morning coffee. They are also called "dunking" biscuits. *Melomakarona* is one of the classic cookies served during Christmas and New Year's. They are made with flour and walnuts and dipped in honey syrup. *Kourabiedes* — almond shortbread cookies dusted with confectioners' sugar — are also served during the winter holidays. Butter-based *koulourakia* come in a variety of shapes and are generally served at Easter.

Greek Biscotti
"Paximadia"

The Italians have biscotti; the Greeks have paximadia. These twice-baked cookies are typically dunked in coffee or wine. Paximadia made with whole wheat flour are harder than these which are made with white flour.

1 cup butter

½ cup vegetable oil

2½ cups sugar

3 eggs plus 1 beaten egg

1 shot ouzo

1½ teaspoons vanilla

½ cup chopped walnuts

½ cup raisins

1 teaspoon baking powder

1 teaspoon baking soda

6 cups flour

Preheat oven to 350°.

Cream butter and oil well in a large mixing bowl. Add 2 cups sugar and mix. Slowly add 3 eggs, ouzo, and vanilla. Add walnuts, raisins, baking powder, and baking soda. Add flour and mix just until the dough comes together.

Shape into 4 loaves and place on sheet tray. Brush with beaten egg and top with remaining ½ cup sugar.

Bake until golden brown, about 25 minutes. Remove from oven. Slice loaves into ¾-inch pieces and return to oven and bake until golden, about another 20 minutes longer.

Yields 20 cookies

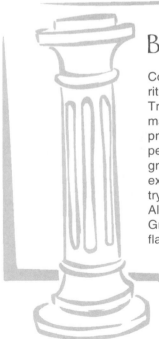

Big Fat Greek Fact

Coffee used to have a major, almost ritualistic, place in the popular culture. Traditional Greeks had the luxury of a coffee master, called a *tambi*, to specifically prepare their individual coffee orders to perfection, down to even the number of grains preferred in their drink. Such expertise may be difficult to find today, so try making your own special recipe at home. All you need is a *briki* (special coffee pot), Greek coffee, sugar, a demitasse cup, and a flame.

Baklava

Baklava is the Greek dessert that everyone knows. It has been a favorite Greek pastry for centuries and is one of the sweetest desserts I know. Some customers at the diner tell me that they can't finish one piece because it is so sweet. You be the judge of that.

3 pounds walnuts, chopped

2 cups sugar

1 pound sweet butter, melted

2 teaspoons cinnamon

2 packages phyllo dough, about 20 sheets of phyllo

8 cups Sweet Dessert Syrup (Recipe appears on page 95.)

Preheat oven to 350°.

Mix together walnuts, sugar, ½ cup melted butter, and cinnamon in a bowl.

Butter a 13 x 9-inch baking pan. Brush 5 sheets of phyllo dough with melted butter and cover the bottom of the pan with them. Cover with a thin layer of walnut mixture. Continue layering until you have 4 layers of phyllo and 3 of the nut mixture. (Top layer should be phyllo.)

Brush the top with melted butter. With a sharp knife, cut the top phyllo sheet into triangles (cutting diagonally across the pan). Bake for about 1½ hours or until phyllo is golden brown.

Remove from oven and pour sweet dessert syrup over the baklava while it is still very hot so that it penetrates into the layers and covers the top. Let cool before serving.

Yields approximately 28 pieces

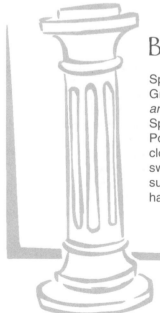

Big Fat Greek Fact

Special foods are served during Christmas in Greece. Desserts such as *baklava* and *amygdalota* are symbolic of good fortune. Specific ingredients have special meanings. Pomegranates, walnuts, chestnuts, and cloves signify prosperity and fertility. White sweets — those covered with powdered sugar and blanched almonds — denote happiness and purity.

Honey Puffs
"Loukoumathes"

Loukoumathes are round fritters. According to the ancient poet, Callimachus, loukoumathes were given as prizes to the winning athletes of the night festivals of games. In Greece they are sometimes served on piles of fig leaves and drizzled with honey and dusted with cinnamon. A dollop of thick creamy Greek yogurt is offered on the side.

2 packages dry yeast

2 cups warm water

4 cups flour

1 teaspoon salt

1 teaspoon vegetable oil

1 tablespoon Metaxa (Greek cognac)

Vegetable oil for frying

Sweet Dessert Syrup (Recipe appears on page 95.)

2 teaspoons cinnamon

Dissolve yeast in a mixing bowl with 1 cup of warm water. Add 1 cup of flour and mix to form a dough. Set dough aside and allow time to rise.

After the dough rises, add remaining water and flour and mix into a batter. Stir in salt, oil, and Metaxa and cover until batter starts to bubble.

Place 2 inches of oil in a deep frying pan or pot. Heat oil to 360°. Use a large spoon to drop batter into hot oil. When golden brown on both sides, remove with a slotted spoon and drain on paper towels. Repeat with remaining batter.

Top with sweet dessert syrup and cinnamon. Serve immediately.

Yields approximately 60 puffs

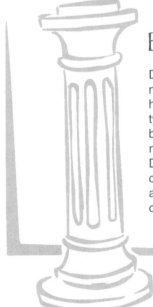

Big Fat Greek Fact

Despite its small size, Greece is one of the most suitable places for the production of honey. The quality of honey depends on the type of plant or flower visited by the bee. The best honey comes from thyme, lavender, and rosemary plants, and lime and orange trees. Due to the country's rich flora and temperate climate, Greek honey has supreme quality and unique physical and chemical characteristics.

Easy Greek Chocolate Cake
"Pasta"

Everyone likes chocolate cake, but they'll love this one. A Greek pasta is known for being very sweet, but very good. This is a must try, but only try a little because it is sweet.

CHOCOLATE CREAM FROSTING

8 ounces cream cheese

3 tablespoons milk

2 tablespoons butter, softened

1½ teaspoons vanilla extract

1 teaspoon orange flavoring

3⅓ cups sifted powdered sugar

¾ cup unsweetened cocoa

⅛ teaspoon salt

Cooking spray

CAKE

1¾ cups all-purpose flour

⅔ cup granulated sugar

⅔ cup packed dark brown sugar

½ cup unsweetened cocoa

1½ teaspoons baking powder

½ teaspoon baking soda

½ teaspoon salt

1 cup milk

½ cup vegetable shortening

2 tablespoons orange flavoring

3 teaspoons vanilla extract

3 large eggs

2 cups Sweet Dessert Syrup (Recipe appears on page 95.)

Cream all frosting ingredients together. Refrigerate.

Preheat oven to 350°. Coat two 8-inch-round cake pans with cooking spray and reserve.

Combine all cake ingredients in a mixing bowl and mix with an electric mixer on first speed for 5 minutes and then on second speed for 3 minutes.

Pour batter into prepared pans and bake for 30 minutes or until cake springs back when touched lightly in center. Cool for 5 minutes, then remove from cake pans.

Place 1 cake layer on a plate. Generously brush with dessert syrup and spread with ½ cup of frosting. Top with remaining cake layer and brush with more dessert syrup. Spread remaining frosting on sides and top of cake.

Refrigerate to let frosting set.

Serves 12

Walnut Cake

"Karythopita"

This cake is a traditional Greek dessert that is also popular throughout Turkey and Armenia.

2½ cups finely ground walnuts

1 cup flour, sifted

2 teaspoons baking powder

1 teaspoon ground cinnamon

⅛ teaspoon ground cloves

6 tablespoons melted butter

¼ cup sugar

4 eggs, separated

1 teaspoon orange flavoring

1 teaspoon brandy

Sweet Dessert Syrup (Recipe appears below.)

Preheat oven 350°. Grease a 13 x 9-inch baking pan.

Mix together walnuts, flour, baking powder, cinnamon, and cloves in a bowl. In a separate bowl whip together butter and sugar. Slowly add egg yolks and mix until fluffy. Continue mixing and add orange flavoring and brandy. Slowly add walnut mixture.

In a separate bowl whip egg whites into a meringue or soft peaks. Fold meringue into walnut mixture.

Pour mixture into prepared pan. Bake about 45 minutes until golden brown.

Remove from oven and IMMEDIATELY drench cake with Greek dessert syrup while cake is piping hot. (There is no exact amount of syrup to use. I use one batch. You might like your cake to be more or less sweet.)

Let cool. Cut into squares or diamonds and serve.

Serves 15 to 20

Sweet Dessert Syrup

This syrup is a staple in Greek dessert cooking. It can be used in all the dessert recipes and can be made and held for an indefinite time.

1 cup fine sugar

½ cup honey

¾ cup water

1 cinnamon stick

4 cloves

3 orange rinds

1 lemon rind

Simmer all ingredients over medium heat until mixture reduces to a syrup state.

Let cool and strain.

Yields approximately 1½ cups

Greek Custard Dessert
"Galatoboureko"

This is one of my wife's favorite desserts, but only if it is made the "right" way. She'll say it has to be a soft creamy custard — but not too soft — and I never get it quite right for her. Experiment with this recipe to find out how you like it. For a thicker custard, add another egg. For a looser custard, add a splash more milk. Enjoy.

2½ cups sugar

¾ cup Farina®

¼ cup cornstarch

10 eggs, beaten

2 quarts milk

2 teaspoons vanilla

1 orange peel

12 sheets phyllo dough

¾ pound sweet butter, melted

4 cups Sweet Dessert Syrup
(Recipe appears on page 95.)

Heat first 7 ingredients in a saucepan. Stir until mixture thickens and begins to boil. Remove from heat and let cool. Remove orange peel.

Preheat oven to 350°.

Layer half the phyllo dough in the bottom of a 13 x 9-inch baking pan, brushing the top of each sheet with melted butter. Pour milk mixture over the phyllo. Cover mixture with remaining phyllo dough, brushing each layer with butter.

Cut into triangles or squares and bake for 50 minutes or until golden brown.

Pour cold sweet desert syrup over custard. Serve cold.

Serves approximately 8 to 12

Big Fat Greek Fact

Phyllo dough is used in many classic Greek dishes such as *spanikopita*. Ancient Greeks believed that a potential bride was not ready to marry until she could roll phyllo dough so thin that her groom could easily read the newspaper through it.

Rice Pudding
"Rizogalo"

My grandfather used to make the best rice pudding. Although it was a long time ago since I've had his, I remember it like it was yesterday. I am sorry that I can not give out his recipe, (which is a secret) but this one is a close second. For those who like a thicker pudding, add one more egg.

1 cup rice
½ cup boiling water
¼ teaspoon salt
8 cups milk
1 cup sugar
3 teaspoons vanilla extract
1 lemon peel
1 orange peel
2 eggs
2 teaspoons cinnamon

Place rice, water, and salt in a pot and simmer for about 5 minutes. Add milk, sugar, vanilla, lemon peel, and orange peel and simmer until rice is tender.

Beat eggs. Add a little of the hot mixture into the eggs and whisk to combine. Pour the eggs into the hot mixture and stir to combine well. (This is called "tempering" and will keep the eggs from scrambling.)

Remove peels and pour mixture into a nice serving pan. Top with cinnamon. Refrigerate until mixture sets and is cold.

Serves 6 to 8

Sauces

Greek-style Red Pepper Coulis

This sauce is great. Use it to dress up fish, chicken, beef, or even vegetables. Your palate will love it no matter what it's on.

1 cup vegetable oil

4 red peppers, trimmed, seeded, and cut into strips

1 clove garlic

½ cup water

¼ teaspoon each salt and pepper

1 sprig fresh oregano

Heat oil in a pot. Add peppers and garlic and cook until softened. Add water, salt and pepper, and oregano. Bring to boil and cook until peppers are very soft.

Remove oregano. Transfer mixture to a blender. Puree into a sauce.

Yields 3 cups

Roasted Red Pepper Sauce

I love how simple this recipe is. You can even use jarred peppers to make it easier. Serve this colorful, flavorful sauce with tortilla chips, fish, chicken, or pasta.

2 tablespoons olive oil

1 clove garlic

1 teaspoon tomato paste

¼ cup dry white wine

4 roasted red peppers, peeled and seeded

1 tablespoon butter

1 teaspoon red pepper flakes

Place all ingredients in a blender and puree until smooth. (More oil might be needed in order to get the thickness desired.)

Yields 2 cups

Greek Tomato Sauce

This is the meatless version of Kima sauce which appears on page 102. Keep some frozen for whenever you need a versatile sauce to perk up your meals.

2 tablespoons oil

1 onion, finely chopped

3 cloves garlic, minced

1 cinnamon stick

1 bay leaf

½ teaspoon chopped mint leaves

1 teaspoon sugar

¼ teaspoon each salt and pepper

3 ounces tomato paste

½ cup red wine

3½ cups water

2 cups crushed tomatoes

Heat oil in a pot, then sauté onions and garlic. When onions are transparent, add cinnamon stick, bay leaf, mint, sugar, and salt and pepper. Cook for 2 minutes, mixing well. Add tomato paste and let caramelize for a couple minutes.

Deglaze with red wine. Add water and crushed tomatoes. Let simmer for 30 minutes.

Yields 8 cups

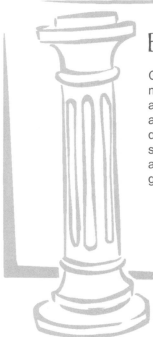

Big Fat Greek Fact

Greek cooks use onions and other members of the onion family, such as leeks and scallions, more as a seasoning than as a vegetable. Onions — fresh or a variety of dried — are added to sauces, stews, and stuffed dishes but are rarely the lone star of any dish. Onions are also eaten raw as a garnish and in salads.

Kima Sauce

This is one of the first recipes I learned how to make. My grandmother sat me down and dictated how she made her sauce, and then we made it together. Throughout the years I have made this sauce hundreds of times and even though it tastes great, it isn't Grandma's.

2 tablespoons oil
½ pound ground beef
1 onion, finely chopped
3 cloves garlic, minced
1 cinnamon stick
1 bay leaf
½ teaspoon chopped mint leaves
1 teaspoon sugar
¼ teaspoon each salt and pepper
3 ounces tomato paste
3½ cups water
2 cups crushed tomatoes

Heat oil in a pot, then sauté ground beef, onion, and garlic. When beef is browned and onions are transparent, add cinnamon stick, bay leaf, mint, sugar, and salt and pepper. Cook for 2 minutes, mixing well. Add tomato paste and let caramelize for a couple minutes.

Deglaze with water. Add crushed tomatoes. Let simmer for 30 minutes to 1 hour.

Yields 10 cups

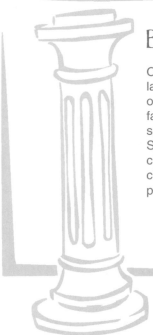

Big Fat Greek Fact

Cinnamon is the dried bark of various laurel trees in the *cinnamomun* family and one of the oldest spices known. It is a favorite ingredient in Greek baked goods, spoon sweets, and custard desserts. Savory dishes, too, benefit from cinnamon. Greek cooks use it to season chicken and lamb dishes, tomato sauces, pilafs, stews, and layered main dishes.

Krema

Krema is a thick béchamel sauce used as a topping on Greek lasagna or as a base to a number of other dishes. It also makes a great Alfredo sauce: just add more milk and a lot more Parmesan cheese.

6 tablespoons butter

¾ cup flour

1 quart hot milk

2 tablespoons Parmesan cheese

2 egg yolks

⅛ teaspoon white pepper

Pinch nutmeg

Melt butter in a saucepot. Add flour and stir. (This makes a blond roux.)

Add hot milk and whisk rapidly so no lumps are formed. Add cheese, egg yolks, white pepper, and nutmeg. (Tempering egg yolks is recommended. To temper, add a little hot liquid to yolks, then add to sauce. This will keep yolks from scrambling.)

Constantly stir so sauce doesn't stick to the bottom of the pot. Bring sauce to a simmer and remove from heat.

Yields ½ gallon

Roux

A roux is a great thickening agent and can be used in gravies or sauces. There are different uses and types of roux. A blond roux is used for lighter gravies, and a dark roux is used for darker sauces or Creole cooking. The only difference between the two is that the dark roux is cooked longer and becomes darker in color.

1 pound butter

3 cups flour, approximately

Melt butter in small pot. When butter has melted, add flour slowly until no butter is left loose and the mixture all balls up together. (Some flour may be left over or more might be needed. This is a sight recipe; however, it can not be messed up.)

Mix constantly until flour has cooked down.

Herb and Spice Substitutions

This has happened to me...I'm in the middle of making a dish and realize I don't have one of the herbs or spices mentioned in the recipe. What do I do? Substitute! Generally 1 tablespoon of finely cut herbs can be substituted for 1 teaspoon dried. Beyond that, this chart will help you choose other alternatives. It's great to experiment but remember that substituting an herb or spice will change the originally intended flavor of the recipe. For this reason, I recommend that you use less of the substitute herb or spice than the recipe calls for. You can always add more and adjust the recipe to your personal taste.

Ingredient	Substitute
Basil	Oregano or Thyme
Chervil	Tarragon or Parsley
Chive	Green Onion; Onion; or Leek
Cilantro	Parsley
Italian Seasoning	Combination of Basil, Oregano, Rosemary, and Ground Red Pepper
Marjoram	Basil; Thyme; or Savory
Mint	Basil; Marjoram; or Rosemary
Oregano	Thyme or Basil
Parsley	Chervil or Cilantro
Poultry Seasoning	Sage plus a Combination of Thyme, Marjoram, Savory, Black Pepper, and/or Rosemary
Red Pepper	Bottled Hot Pepper Sauce or Black Pepper
Rosemary	Thyme; Tarragon; or Savory
Sage	Poultry Seasoning; Savory; Marjoram; or Rosemary
Savory	Thyme; Marjoram; or Sage
Tarragon	Chervil or Aniseed
Thyme	Basil; Marjoram; Oregano; or Savory
Allspice	Cinnamon; Cassia; Nutmeg; Mace; or Cloves
Aniseed	Fennel Seed or Anise Extract
Cardamom	Ginger
Chili Powder	Bottled Hot Pepper Sauce plus Oregano and Cumin
Cinnamon	Nutmeg or Allspice (use no more than half the original amount)
Cloves	Allspice; Cinnamon; or Nutmeg
Cumin	Chili Powder
Ginger	Allspice; Cinnamon; Mace; or Nutmeg
Mace	Allspice; Cinnamon; Ginger; or Nutmeg
Nutmeg	Cinnamon; Ginger; or Mace
Saffron	Turmeric

General Cooking Substitutions

If your recipe calls for:	Substitute
Baking powder (1 teaspoon)	¼ teaspoon baking soda and ½ teaspoon cream of tartar
Catsup (1 cup)	1 cup tomato sauce, ½ cup sugar, and 2 tablespoons vinegar (for use in cooking)
Chocolate chips, semisweet (1 ounce)	1 ounce sweet cooking chocolate
Chocolate, unsweetened (1 ounce)	3 tablespoons cocoa and 1 tablespoon fat
Coconut milk (1 cup)	1 cup whole milk
Corn syrup (1 cup)	1 cup sugar and ¼ cup liquid (use whatever liquid is called for in the recipe)
Cornstarch, 1 tablespoon	2 tablespoons all-purpose flour or 2 tablespoons granulated tapioca
Cream, heavy (1 cup)	¾ cup milk and ⅓ cup butter or margarine
Cream, light (1 cup)	¾ cup milk and 3 tablespoons butter or margarine
Egg (1 whole)	2 yolks and 1 tablespoon water (in cookies) OR 2 yolks (in custards, fillings, and similar mixtures) OR 2 whites
Flour, all-purpose (1 tablespoon)	1½ teaspoons cornstarch or arrowroot starch 1 tablespoon granular tapioca
Honey (1 cup)	1¼ cups sugar and ¼ cup liquid (use liquid called for in recipe)
Horseradish (1 tablespoon fresh)	2 tablespoons bottled
Lemon juice (1 teaspoon)	½ teaspoon vinegar
Mayonnaise (1 cup)	½ cup yogurt and ½ cup mayonnaise OR 1 cup cottage cheese pureed in blender
Milk, buttermilk (1 cup)	1 cup plain yogurt
Milk, whole (1 cup)	1 cup reconstituted non-fat dry milk and 2 teaspoons butter or margarine OR ½ cup evaporated milk and ½ cup water
Nuts (1 cup)	1 cup rolled oats, browned (in baked products)
Sour cream (1 cup)	1 cup plain yogurt
Sugar, brown (1 cup firmly packed)	1 cup granulated sugar OR 1 cup granulated sugar plus ¼ cup molasses
Sugar, white (1 cup)	1 cup corn syrup, decrease liquid called for in recipe by ¼ cup (never replace more than ½ cup sugar called for in recipe with corn syrup)
Tomato sauce	¾ cup tomato paste plus 1 cup water
Vanilla bean (½ bean)	1 tablespoon vanilla extract
Worcestershire sauce (1 teaspoon)	1 teaspoon bottled steak sauce
Yogurt, plain (1 cup)	1 cup sour cream

Index

Index

Index

Index

Index

Order Form

Please send me _____ copies of My Big Fat Greek Feast Cookbook at $15.95 per copy.

_____ Book amount total
_____ Sales tax: New Jersey addresses, please add $.90 per book
_____ Shipping: $2.50 for the first book; $1.00 for each additional book
_____ Total amount enclosed

Name: _____

Address: _____

City/State/Zip _____

Phone _____ E-mail _____

Checks and money orders are accepted for payment.

Please send this form and payment to:

George Kyrtatas
7 Tidewater Court
Hainesport, NJ 08036

Thank you !

About the Author

George Kyrtatas discovered his passion for cooking at a young age. From early childhood George would watch cooking programs with his dad. Whether it was "Julia Child" or "The Frugal Gourmet," he would watch. In 1986, George's parents, Antonia and Evangelos (Angelo), opened Hathaway's Restaurant in Cinnaminson, N.J. George began learning how to work and how to cook "professionally" at a young age.

As the years went by, George knew he wanted to be in the restaurant business; he wanted to be a great chef. When it was time to go to college, George went to the Academy of Culinary Arts in May's Landing, N.J. George already knew how to cook, but there he learned the principles of cooking.

At the age of 20, George had worked with some of the great chefs of our time. He cooked with Martin Yan and Curtis Atkins and did the prep work for the taping of "Emeril Live" in Philadelphia, to name a few. That same year George was inducted into the American Culinary Federation as a Certified Chef de Cuisine and graduated from The Academy of Culinary Arts with a Gold Medal in the culinary program and with an Associates Degree in Applied Science from Atlantic Cape Community College. At 21, George married the love of his life. Now at the age of 24, George and his wife Fran are ecstatically awaiting their first child.

George can be found most of the time at his second home, Hathaway's Restaurant. George and his brother are now partners in the business that their parents made successful. Hathaway's is a 280-seat diner with a Sports Bar. There you can eat the best food in the area. Hathaway's has everything from eggs all day to sauté specialties, steak, and seafood. Hathaway's occasionally serves a traditional Greek meal. Everything at Hathaway's is made fresh and from scratch to ensure its customers the greatest meal. Stop in and say hi to Chef George and eat some of the great food at Hathaway's.